Nostalgia

Nostalgia

WHEN ARE WE EVER AT HOME?

Barbara Cassin

Translated by

PASCALE-ANNE BRAULT

FORDHAM UNIVERSITY PRESS

New York 2016

Nostalgia was first published in French under the title *La nostalgie:
Quand donc est-on chez soi? Ulysse, Énée, Arendt* by Éditions Autrement,
Collection Les Grands Mots, © Autrement, Paris, 2013.

This work, published as part of a program providing publication assistance,
received financial support from the French Ministry of Foreign Affairs, the
Cultural Services of the French Embassy in the United States and FACE (French
American Cultural Exchange). French Voices Logo designed by Serge Bloch.

Ouvrage publié avec le concours du Ministère français chargé
de la Culture–Centre National du Livre.

This work has been published with the assistance of the French Ministry
of Culture–National Center for the Book.

Fordham University Press also publishes its books in a variety
of electronic formats. Some content that appears in print may not
be available in electronic books.

Visit us online at www.fordhampress.com.

Printed and bound in Great Britain by
Marston Book Services Ltd, Oxfordshire

18 17 16   5 4 3 2 1

First edition

(Copyright page continued on page 79.)

Staying as I am,

One foot in one country and the other in another,

I find my condition to be very happy, in that it is free.

—René Descartes, Letter to Elisabeth of Bohemia, July 1648

CONTENTS

FOREWORD

Souleymane Bachir Diagne

To the question "When are we ever at home?" Barbara Cassin offers here three answers represented by three figures, the first two mythical and the last one real: Odysseus, Aeneas, and Hannah Arendt. The first character, Odysseus, who is characterized as "divine," answers the question by continuously deferring his "being back home": even when he finally gets there and joins his wife Penelope in the very bed he sculpted himself out of a living tree, making sure it would thus remain rooted and unmovable, he is again driven away after only three days by his very incapacity to *inhabit* a home. What his Odyssey teaches him—and us—is that "home is the Mediterranean," meaning the open, the cosmic, the infinite . . .

The journey of the second figure, Aeneas, known as the pious, apparently is the opposite of Odysseus's: he leaves his native city of Troy in flames, taking with him what he can of his homeland, symbolized primarily by his father, whom he carries on his back. But he is not so much leaving a destroyed home as traveling toward the foundation of a new city, which is to become the center of the known world. And the most important aspect of that journey toward foundation, we discover with him, is that home is the new language, Latin, that he now adopts: instead of performing the colonial and imperial gesture of imposing new names and his Greek language on the natives, he melts into the local language and *inhabits* it as his home.

For the real historical figure too, Hannah Arendt, home is the language that she lives in against all opposition. Unlike Aeneas, who gave consent to his new home, Latin, the philosopher kept inhabiting her native tongue in spite of her exile: the German language was what remained of a homeland, or rather, what remained *as* a homeland. In so doing she taught us that

ix

there is a "difference between the mother tongue and the land of the fathers." Commenting on Arendt on that point, Barbara Cassin proposes here an important distinction between the language that we put into work as *energeia*, in which we allow ourselves to make radically new possibilities happen because we feel that we contribute to its continuous creation, and the language that we use, no matter how well we master it, as " a static totality," which we perceive as already constituted outside of us, as an *ergon*.

But even if the mother tongue stands apart because of the unique way in which we inhabit it, it is still "one language among others." That phrase, the experience of discovering that our language is "one language among others," is at the core of Barbara Cassin's philosophy of language (or rather languages), to which this book constitutes an excellent introduction. Although the topic of language does not appear explicitly in Barbara Cassin's reading of the *Odyssey*, it is implicitly present, as the subsequent chapters on Aeneas and Arendt make clear in retrospect. In fact, this precise and beautifully written exploration of the meaning of "nostalgia" (well served by the translation) is, throughout, as is the whole work of Barbara Cassin, a meditation on languages in their *plurality* and their *equivalence*, and on *translation*. When we fully understand that we do not speak the *logos*, and when we authentically experience that our language is just "one language among others," then we are ready to philosophize otherwise, to philosophize between languages, or, in Cassin's words, to "philosophize in tongues." That is the program of research around which this leading figure of contemporary French philosophy has now gathered many scholars from all over the world. As an invitation to a voyage.

TRANSLATOR'S NOTE

I would like to thank Veronica Lalov for her invaluable work tracking down references and express my gratitude to the College of Liberal Arts and Social Sciences at DePaul University for their support of this project. Finally, this translation owes much to the excellent suggestions provided by Michael Naas and Elizabeth Rottenberg.

Whenever possible, I have used published translations for the citations. I have, however, made occasional changes to follow more closely Cassin's language and argument.

Nostalgia

Of Corsican Hospitality

It has been found again. What has?—Eternity.
It is the sea gone off with the sun.

—ARTHUR RIMBAUD[1]

An Island, at Home, Not at Home

It looks like I'm going home, but it's not home. Maybe it's because I have
no home. Or maybe it's because it's when I'm not home that I feel most at
home, in a place that feels like home. When are we ever at home?

I get off the plane and pick up the car in the airport parking lot. They
tell me where to find my trusty old white Peugeot, with the Paris license
plates still on it, which drives like a truck. I get on the road. It's summer, so
I take the road that runs along the lagoon, among the fruits and vegetables,
the large lemons, cantaloupes, watermelons, apricots, and the early figs,
the beefsteak tomatoes, the purple-veined eggplants, the small thick zuc-
chinis. Tunnels, rotaries, speed bumps, and turns, one after the other. The
road moves in and out. The turns have become one with my hands, which
are so easily distracted, one with the steering wheel itself. Beyond the
exhaust fumes, the seasons bring smells of the maquis ("the faintest hint of

pines, a touch of tarragon," says the prisoner in *Asterix* who has just escaped),[2] mimosa, oleander, fire, and sea. I notice the expansion of the industrial zone, new and restored houses; there are fewer changes as soon as one is on the cape road. Like a horse on the way to its stables, I'm going home.

It is with this experience that I wish to begin: the feeling I inwardly qualify as an irrepressible nostalgia and that I experience every time I'm "back" in Corsica. A strange feeling, since my ancestors are not from this island; I wasn't born there, and I didn't spend either my childhood or my youth there. I'm not Corsican. I was born in Paris; that's where I live and work. I had my children there and brought them up in a charming house, even if it's a bit dark, in the center of Paris. I've got the high-pitched accent of a *pinzutu*.[3] Why, then, do I feel so strongly that I am returning home? How is it that I can miss it to this extent whenever I am away for a long time, always for too long? "You've come back to *te ressourcer*"—to be rejuvenated, to replenish your resources—they often tell me in the village. But what a strange French expression: what sources? What resources? I'm not at home, yet I am. Just as the Gospel speaks of "those who use the world, as though they did not make full use of it" (1 Corinthians 7:31), I am at home "as though," or insofar as, I am not at home. It is because I have no roots there that the uprooted one that I am, which I like to be and hope to remain (my mother was of Hungarian-Jewish descent by way of Trieste and the irredentist lands,[4] and my father's family, descended from barbarian pirates, supposedly acted as one of the pope's bankers in the Comtat Venaissin), finds herself "as though" at home.

I wanted to reflect on and dream of nostalgia because, obviously, I love Homer, Odysseus, the Greek language, and the Mediterranean. But also, and this is a bit stranger, because I am attached to Corsica, to the horizon of a house, a village, a cape on another island, one that is not mine, at least insofar as I wasn't born there. Yet "nostalgia" is the word that naturally comes to mind when I think about it. But as with "Homer" himself, "nostalgia" is not exactly what one believes it to be. Just as Homer is not the original poet, the one and only one to have composed the *Iliad* and the *Odyssey* that we have, nostalgia is not simply homesickness and the return home.[5] This feeling, at once overwhelming and gentle, is, like every origin, a chosen fiction that constantly gives clues so as to be taken for what it is, an adorable, human fiction, a cultural fact. Would the best way to be back home in one's homeland[6] not then be, as in an *Odyssey* transformed by the modern context, to be in a home that is not one's own?

Just like language, a homeland "is not something that belongs."[7]

I would like to begin with an experience that is very personal, too personal.

My husband died after a long and short illness, which was greeted with a gentle resignation in this faraway village, in the space of a house built by us and for us.

Among the extravagant rights of this strange and still Napoleonic territory that is Corsica—in addition, that is, to the rights of inheritance and the price of cigarettes—is the privilege to have a grave in one's home so long as the local authorities allow it. My husband is buried in that village, at that house, on a terrace overlooking the roof, the marina, and the sea. A stone was erected with his name and the dates of his birth and death engraved on it by friends, who took their boat out to look for a stone in a creek. We sit on a bench of driftwood we built together. It is there, next to his, that I have my own grave, which for now still sounds hollow, in a soil that does not belong—ours, not ours. On the day of his death, which was expected though still unknown ("he is so tired, stop looking at him, let him go," the woman doctor told me that morning), the grave was not yet finished. That day, though, two people called to tell me that their family grave would take him in: "that too is Corsican hospitality."

We are, as one might say in French, *hospités*, that is, taken in out of hospitality, hospited. After all, I am French, as it says on my identity papers, and Corsica is in France, so I am simply at home in my country. Yet it is only because I am *hospitée* that I feel at home there. Others have their roots there, deeper roots than I do, and they welcome me. Since I did not inherit any land from my parents, and I am grateful to them for that, I enjoy one piece of land that is not mine first of all, not mine at all, even if I own it legally. For there is reciprocity in the air. A *hôte*: in French the same word designates both the one who welcomes and the one who is welcomed, and that is an immemorial discovery, civilization itself. One should probably add that in Greek the word *xenos*, which means *hôte* in these two senses, also means "stranger," the one who must above all be given hospitality, while in Latin *hostis* also designates "enemy": trust-distrust. Above the house, one can see the tower where Seneca is said to have written *De Consolatione*. We are, dead and alive, *hospités*, given hospitality there, by the village. But we are given hospitality too by the world, in a truly Greek cosmos that unfolds in this horizon so unique to islands: "It has been found again. What has?—Eternity. It is the sea gone off with the sun," Rimbaud lucidly wrote (and those were the words that came to my lips to thank all those, known and sometimes unknown, whose sadness was a show of honor and who came, under the heat of a midday sun in June, to greet the violently jolting hearse).

The reality of an island. An island is real in a way that is very precise. Its edges can be seen from a boat or plane. And, when seen from an island, the maritime horizon bends; in the evening, with the setting sun, the earth is round. When we are in the middle of the water, we know that there is a shore, a limit between an inside and the great outside, and that the island is finite. An island is an entity par excellence, an identity, something with a contour, an *eidos*; it emerges like an idea. In its finitude, an island is a point of view on the world. An island is something that is immersed in the cosmos; it is cosmic and cosmological, with the starry sky above our heads and the immensity before us, visible to the eye. In Greece, as in Corsica, I have repeatedly had the experience of the *cosmos*, the "world" of the Greeks— "order and beauty," says Baudelaire. At each bend in the road, at each turn, at each step, the world gets recomposed and reorganized. What the eye sees at that very moment becomes structure; the eye is seized by harmony, each time astonished anew. Between cosmology and cosmetics, the horizon, at once immense and limited, renews its order. An island is a place par excellence.

The nostalgia for an island. An island is a place, but a very singular place, a place that invites departure: one can only leave an island, "O Death, old Captain."[8] And one wants to return; one must return to it. It determines and magnetizes. One begins to believe that time bends like the horizon and that one will return after a long journey, a cycle, an odyssey.

But do we ever really return? And do we ever really remain there?

Nostalgia, a Swiss Word

"Nostalgia": the word sounds perfectly Greek, made up of *nostos*, "return," and *algos*, "pain," "suffering." Nostalgia is the "pain of return," both the suffering that has a hold on you when you are far away and the pains you must endure in order to return. The *Odyssey*, which, together with the *Iliad*, founds Greek language and culture, is the epic of a blind poet, "Homer," who in all likelihood never existed. He composed this epic in order to sing of the adventures of Odysseus's return, the hero of a thousand ruses. It is the poem of nostalgia par excellence.

Yet "nostalgia" is not a Greek word. It is not found in the *Odyssey*. It is not Greek but Swiss, Swiss-German. It is, to be exact, the name of an illness first classified as such in the seventeenth century. It was invented, if we are to believe the *Historical Dictionary of the French Language*, in 1678, by a doctor, Jean-Jacques Harder, to describe the homesickness, *Heimweh*, from which Louis XIV's faithful and costly ("no money, no Swiss") Swiss mercenaries suffered. Unless it was coined in 1688 by Johans or Jean Hofer, the son of an Alsatian minister from Mulhouse, who, at the age of nineteen, devoted a short doctoral thesis to this condition at the University of Basel in order to describe the illness suffered by certain "young people." Among these was a young man from Bern who was studying in Basel and who was getting sicker by the day but who recovered his health upon his return to Bern, indeed even before getting there. There was also the case of a peasant woman who had been hospitalized ("Ich will heim, ich will heim," she would moan, refusing all medication and food) and was then cured once back home—the origin recognizable by its telling symptoms.[9]

Right away it became a military question: the Swiss would desert whenever they heard the "ranz of the cows," the song or air from the Alpine pastures, a "celebrated Air," as Rousseau writes in his *Dictionary of Music*, that "was so generally beloved among the Swiss that it was forbidden to be play'd in their troops under pain of death, because it made those who heard it burst into tears, desert, or die, so great a desire did it excite in them of returning to their country."[10]

And thus, in order to designate an illness suffered by the German-speaking Swiss, the medical profession coined this word "nostalgia," just as one talks of "myalgia" or "neuralgia." If I insist on this, it is because the origin of this word seems to me very representative of what an origin is: this word, which evokes the entire *Odyssey*, has nothing original or originary about it; in short, there is nothing "Greek" about it. It is fabricated, historically crossbred (and since an origin is precisely not a fact of history, we should say here "historially," to borrow a term coined by Heidegger) and serves, as do all origins, a retrospective finality. The typography used in the *Dissertatio de nostalgia* is proof of this, with its Latin capital letters for DISSERTATIO MEDICA, its Greek capital letters for the coined word ΝΟΣΤΑΛΓΙΑ, and, in gothic small caps, *oder Heimweh*, "homesickness." The term was almost eclipsed by *philopatridomania* ("the madness of love for one's homeland"), which was also put forward by Harder, and by *pothopatridalgia* ("the suffering from the desire-passion for one's home-land"), a term coined by Zwinger, and by the subtitle *Heimsehnsucht*, given by Haller . . . But it is *nostos*, "the return," that won out. Consulting the Chantraine dictionary does not add much this time: *nostos* comes from *neomai*, meaning "to come back, to return"; it is derived from a root whose meaning in the active voice would be "to save." *Anostos* means "without return, bearing no fruit"; *Nestor* is the name of "he who fortunately returns, who fortunately brings his army back"; and, in modern Greek, *nostimos* means "tasty, sweet." The likely meaning of the root is "fortunate return, salvation." We find it in the Germanic languages, in Anglo-Saxon ("to be cured, saved, to survive," and "to save, to cure, to nourish"). Sanskrit has words corresponding to *neomai*, for example, *nasate*, "to approach, to join," this slight difference in meaning posing no serious problem here; one might want to compare it to *nimsate*, "they kiss, touch with the mouth." Return and love are not unconnected.

This book questions, together with "nostalgia," the relationship between homeland or fatherland, exile, and mother tongue. The *Odyssey*, which recounts the adventures of Odysseus and his endlessly delayed return, is the very poem of nostalgia. The so very symbolic sign that Odysseus is finally "home," in his homeland, is his bed, which is rooted, carved with his own hands from out of an olive tree, around which he built his house, a secret shared only with his wife. Rootedness and uprootedness: that is nostalgia.

As for Aeneas, when he flees Troy in flames, he carries his homeland on his back, his father, Anchises, and his gods of the earth on his shoulders. He wanders from place to place until Juno, who is pursuing him in her hatred, agrees to let him found what will become Rome, but only on one condition: that he forget Greek and speak, as Virgil says, "with one mouth [*uno ore*]," "speaking one tongue," with and as the Latin people (Book XII, 837). The founding epic is also, this time, the founding of a language.

To have one's language for a homeland, or even for one's sole homeland. That is how, in dark times, Hannah Arendt, "naturalized" in her American exile, chooses to define herself: not in relation to a country or a people but only in relation to a language, the German language. It is this language that she misses and wants to hear.

What is proper? What is foreign? "Happy, the man who, like Odysseus": nothing is further from the truth than Du Bellay's sonnet, since Odysseus, upon his return "home," stays but one night, however long that night may seem.[11] Indeed, he must leave again and travel as far as possible from his homeland, as far as possible from the sea. He must walk inland, carrying the oar of a ship, until a man crosses his path and asks him: "What winnowing fan is that upon your shoulder?" (Book XI, 97). Only then can Odysseus plant the oar in the soil, thus making a last offering to Poseidon, the god of the sea, and return to live among his kin for the rest of his life. But the *Odyssey* says nothing about this. For it is rather the "not yet," as well as perhaps the misrecognition that relates the proper to the foreign—this oar that must be mistaken for a winnowing fan—that characterize nostalgia.

In this work, I will analyze the relationship of man to time, to death as well as to eternity, along with his relationship to his homeland, for better and for worse. I will use as background a series of primal scenes that are depicted by Homer and that, to my eyes, define nostalgia. But I will think too about the modern usages of this notion, related to all the ambiguities, sometimes so terrifying, of the at-home and of patriotism, from *home* to *Heimat*, all the way to the cult of the land and blood propagated by Fascism and Nazism. For each language has its own way of saying nostalgia, of locating the malaise in a specific place in the body (*melancholia*: black bile; *spleen*: the spleen; *anxiety*: the throat), so as to inscribe it within a cultural register as a password, even if it is imported, as was *spleen*, from Shakespeare to Baudelaire, to link it, in relation to the past or to the future, to an event or an expectation, to make of it an individual, historical, ontological, religious, social, or patriotic illness—*acedia, dor, saudade, Sehnsucht, desengaño*, etc.[12] I will ask if and how it is possible to rework this relation between nostalgia and the native land or patriotism, in order to make of nostalgia a completely different adventure, one that would lead us to the threshold of a much broader and more welcoming way of thinking, to a vision of the world freed from all belonging. Or else: in what way, in what ways, can we say that nostalgia is a feeling that defines Europe?—"European: one who is nostalgic for Europe,"[13] says Kundera in *The Art of the Novel*.

Odysseus and the Day of Return

"What man has put my bed in another place?"

—HOMER, *The Odyssey* (XXIII, 184)

The Rooted Bed

THE MORTAL CONDITION

The return of Odysseus is as paradoxical as the nostalgia invented by the Swiss. For when Odysseus finally reaches the land of Ithaca, he does not recognize it, and he himself is at first recognized only by his dog. And when he wins back his identity, after having massacred the suitors and unfaithful attendants, when he finds his wife again and she consents to recognize him at last, the hero stays only for a night and then leaves again.

Odysseus had left his island seventeen years earlier, if I am counting correctly. It took ten years for all the Greek warriors to retrieve Helen, taken away by Paris, and to bring Troy to its knees. At the end of ten years, those who had not died returned home, sometimes, like Agamemnon, only to find treachery and their destiny. But Odysseus continued not to return.

The question raised by the *Odyssey* is whether Odysseus, the only one of the survivors not to have returned home, is "returnable," *nostimos* in Greek, whether he is ever going to know "the day of return," *nostimon ēmar*, or whether this has been taken "away" (I, 9), whether his day of homecoming "has perished" or been "lost" (I, 168, 354).[1]

> Then all the others, as many as fled sheer destruction, were at home
> now, having escaped the sea and the fighting. This one alone, longing
> for his wife and his homecoming, was detained by the queenly nymph
> Calypso, bright among goddesses, in her hollowed caverns, desiring
> that he should be her husband. (I, 11–15)[2]

The poem opens in the middle of the action, with an assembly of the gods that shows the intimate relationship between men and gods, the immanence of men-gods from the side of the gods, an immanence that constitutes, in my view, the marvel of paganism. The reciprocal situation is expressed from the side of men in this way by René Char: "We are not jealous of the gods, we neither serve them nor fear them, but in peril of our lives we attest to their multiple existences, and are moved at belonging to their adventurous breed that no longer remembers them."[3]

A few words are in order here to give some sense of the pagan world that Homer has us enter. As Nietzsche says, "it makes a difference whether Homer or the Bible or science tyrannizes human beings."[4] Here is the criterion I would suggest to define the pagan world: it is a world in which the one who arrives before you might always be a god, for that is what a pagan expects when he meets a human being: he or she may be divine. In a monotheistic world, that could not happen—even if the Messiah has already come. In Homer's world, on the contrary, everything is permeable: men, gods, animals, things. Odysseus is the "divine Odysseus" as "naturally" as he is *polutropos*, "of a thousand ruses" (the Homeric epithets are said to be "nature epithets"; they bespeak the "nature," the very being, of what they designate). And when he appears before Nausicaa, he is "like some hill-kept lion." As for Nausicaa, Odysseus addresses her whether she be "mortal or goddess," and he likens her in her incomparable beauty to "the stalk of a young palm" (VI, 130, 149, 163). *Kosmos*, "order and beauty,"

is thus the word to describe this dreamlike harmony of the world, percep-
tible in the always Greek reality of an island. It is not a question, then, of
whether the transcendent God exists or not, either as demiurge or mathe-
matician; the gods are rather the oneiric lining immanent to the world.
These "brilliant Olympians, born of dream," are, for the Greeks, "the
sphere of beauty, in which they saw their mirror images," says Nietzsche,
who suggests characterizing the "dreaming Greeks as Homers and Homer
as a dreaming Greek."[5] Such is the world the *Odyssey* makes us enter. We
will see that it is not quite Virgil's world: between the "divine Odysseus"
and the "pious Aeneas," it is not the same way of being pagan—the one is
"natural," the other "political."

In front of the assembled gods, Athena complains that Odysseus, whom
she protects, is the only one who has not returned home. He, who would
like to see the smoke rise from his land, cries out from afar and calls for
death.

It has been seven years that Calypso, "the one who keeps in hiding,"
"the one who covers over," has kept Odysseus from his island and poured
sweet loving words upon him so that he might forget Ithaca. The nymph is
Poseidon's daughter, the god of the Sea, whom Odysseus offended by kill-
ing the Cyclops and who persists in refusing him his day of return. But
Poseidon is far away, gone to the Ethiopians, and Athena proposes to take
advantage of his absence. Zeus says: "for so it is fated that he shall see his
people and come back to his house" (V, 41). He thus sends Hermes to
Calypso. The nymph with flowing hair responds that she will obey this
decree without protest, though she complains that the jealous gods are
"resentful toward the goddesses for sleeping openly with such men as each
has made her true husband" (V, 119). Love and love rivalries, the relationship between the new and the old, the way the new becomes old and the
novel habit—in short, time as linear and as cyclical—that is one of the
keys to nostalgia.

Here is the central scene that describes homesickness. Calypso, obedient, goes to Odysseus:

> [She] found him sitting on the seashore, and his eyes were never wiped
> dry of tears, and the sweet lifetime was draining out of him [*kateibeto*
> *glukus aiōn*], as he wept for a way home, since the nymph was no longer
> pleasing to him. By nights he would lie beside her, of necessity, in the
> hollow caverns . . . in tears and lamentation and sorrow as he looked
> out over the barren water. (V, 151–158)

We have here the very image of nostalgia à la Caspar David Friedrich:
Odysseus on his promontory, seen from behind, looking out to sea, "his
sweet *aiōn* flowing out of him," the flow of his tears thus dissipating the
"sap" and "time" of his life (for *aiōn* says all of this at once).[6]

Calypso, who is in love with him and is going to help him, warns him
one last time: "I wish you well, however you do it, but if you only knew in
your own heart how many hardships you were fated to undergo before
getting back to your country, you would stay here with me and be the lord
of this household and be an immortal" (V, 205–210).

Nostalgia is what makes one prefer going home, even if it means finding
there a time that passes by, death—and, worse, old age—rather than
immortality. Such is the weight of the desire to return. Odysseus responds
to her:

> Goddess and queen, do not be angry with me. I myself know that all
> you say is true and that circumspect Penelope can never match the
> impression you make for beauty and stature. She is mortal after all,
> and you are immortal and ageless. But even so, what I want and all my
> days I pine for is to go back to my house and see my day of homecom-
> ing. (V, 215–220)

Kant claimed that those suffering from nostalgia, the Swiss included,
are always disappointed because it is not the place of their youth that they
seek but their youth itself—"they find their anticipation dampened" and,
thus, he adds, "their homesickness cured."[7] Odysseus gives proof, rather, to
the contrary: it is Penelope he wants, even with her age. Not eternal youth
but the time that passes. It is true, nostalgia connects space and time. But
it chooses the mortal condition and anchors this condition in a place. Love
elsewhere, the love of elsewhere, yields before the desire for the same.

Rather than the sovereign beauty of Calypso, rather than eternity, nostalgia chooses finitude and *oikade*, home. To return home is to submit to a common fate: aging, dying—living "with one's kin for the rest of one's life," sighs Du Bellay.[8] And when Odysseus leaves for a second time, it is still the return that makes him sigh.

RECOGNITION

But how do you know you are back home?

Odysseus had already come once within sight of Ithaca. He tells the Phaeacians how, after the episode with the Cyclops, he came to the home of Aeolus, the king of winds, who gave him and his companions hospitality. The good-hearted king of the winds wanted to ensure Odysseus's return by getting Zephyr's gentle breath to carry them along and by enclosing the roaring winds in a goatskin, which he entrusted to him. And so, after sailing for nine days and nine nights, the fields of his homeland appeared so close that the men looking after the fires could be seen. "But then sweet sleep came upon me, for I was worn out with always handling the ship myself, and I would not give it to any other companion, so we could come home quicker to our own country" (X, 31–33). He goes to sleep, they open the bag, the winds are unleashed, and they are back to where they began. When Odysseus sees Ithaca from the sea, he recognizes it with clarity, but his sleep makes him lose it again for another eight years, a whole Odyssey—Laestrygonians, Circe, Hades, the Sirens, Scylla and Charybdis, the island of the Sun, Calypso.

This time is thus the second time. Odysseus has left Calypso's island on a raft; he has been shipwrecked as she foretold; exhausted, he has fallen asleep, on the shore, near a river. A ball wakes him up, that of Nausicaa and her attendants, who are playing while the laundry is drying. He begs her ("I am at your knees . . . and terribly afraid to clasp you by the knees" [VI, 141–169], he says, inventing the performative).[9] He comes to the Phaeacians' palace; he is given hospitality, hears the story of the *Iliad* and weeps, before then himself telling the tale of what follows. The Phaeacians, who are good ferrymen but who have incurred the wrath of the god of the Seas, bring him back, all alone, since his comrades have all died, one after the other. They leave him on his island—sound asleep once again, as he often is at crucial moments.

Odysseus, who recognized his island when he was not yet there, now fails to recognize it when he is there. Book XIII is devoted to this inability to recognize, mirrored by the fact that Odysseus must himself go unrecognized, be unrecognizable. "But now great Odysseus wakened from sleep in his own homeland, and he did not know it, having been long away, for the goddess, Pallas Athena, daughter of Zeus, poured a mist over all, so she could make him unrecognizable" (XIII, 187–191).

He is there at last, but he is not at all there; everything is of another form, of another idea (*alloeidos*), and nothing is more terrifyingly strange, *unheimlich*, nothing more uncanny, than his homeland. The Freudian terms are hardly out of place: the homeland, *Heimat*, is *unheimlich*, at home (*heim*) but not at home (*unheim*), the very paradigm of the "uncanny." As Freud says, "The German word *unheimlich* is obviously the opposite of *heimlich* [homely], *heimisch* [native]—the opposite of what is familiar; and we are tempted to conclude that what is 'uncanny' is frightening precisely because it is *not* known and familiar." But that is not at all the case: "the uncanny is that class of the frightening which leads back to what is known of old and long familiar."[10] This is why Victor Bérard, translating no doubt inexactly but with great insight, introduces the term "anxiety," this very particular kind of fear without object that leaves a lump in the throat:

> Therefore to the lord Odysseus she made everything look otherwise than it was, the penetrating roads, the harbors where all could anchor, the rocks going straight up, and the trees tall growing. He sprang and stood upright and looked about at his native country, and groaned aloud and struck himself on both thighs with the flats of his hands, and spoke a word of lamentation [Bérard: *un cri d'angoisse*, a cry of anxiety]: "Ah me, what are the people whose land I have come to this time." (XIII, 194–200)

Odysseus makes a bitter inventory of the rich gifts left beside him: "There was nothing gone from all of this; but he in great sorrow crept over the beach of his own country beside the resounding sea, with much lamentation" (XIII, 219–221). When he is closest, he is farthest away. Absence and mist are combined: there is nothing obvious about the homeland; it is not a proof of itself, it is not an *index sui*, as was sometimes said of God. Athena, in the guise of a beautiful young boy, has to describe it to him and name it: "Ithaca." Then, the gray-eyed goddess, appearing now as a woman, dissipates the mist so that he can finally see the place, the land, the earth, the grain-giving ground (XIII, 344–354).[11] How does one ultimately recognize one's island? One recognizes it, I think, because one is recognized there, that is, because one has one's identity there.

Odysseus's entire journey, the entire *Odyssey*, sails under the aegis of a quest for identity as well as the aegis of nostalgia. The famous episode of the Cyclops, where Odysseus strikes the monster with the phrase "Nobody (*outis*) is my name" (IX, 366), is one of the key moments. Most noteworthy there is the wordplay linked to negation, *outis/mētis*, two ways of saying "nobody" in Greek, except that the second is a homophone of *mētis*, the "ruse" that characterizes Odysseus. Identity is, clearly, a matter of signifiers.[12] Yet the quest for identity becomes, with the return to Ithaca, a process of recognition: the importance of words, of signifiers, both proper and metaphorical, more proper than the proper, then becomes clearer and clearer.

In Ithaca, Odysseus is recognized several times in succession, each time in a very singular way. A key moment, already before Ithaca, serves as a condition and a counterpoint to all the others. It occurs when Odysseus hears his identity as "Odysseus" being sung by the Sirens. He sails past their small island, stopping up his rowers' ears with wax, and he has himself tied to the mast so as not to drown in desire by trying to embrace the Sirens, so as not "to lose his homecoming." He listens to them telling him of the hero he is: "Come this way, honored Odysseus, great glory of the Achaians" (XII, 184). But Odysseus says, "I remain firmly planted in the ground [*empedon autothi mimnō*]" (XII, 161), bound to the mast, within the strictures of a painful bondage that the sailors have been told to tighten even more when it becomes necessary. These words tell of how it is to be recognized, identified: one is "planted in the ground."

Let me leave the *Odyssey* for a moment to show how, with this "planted in the ground," the mytheme, the recurring element of myth, becomes a concept. Let me remind you that this same vocabulary (*empedon authi menei*, "planted in the ground") is used to describe Being in Parmenides' poem, that is, in the great *logos* wherein philosophy begins. The poem invites one to follow "the path of 'is,'" there where Being, thinking, and speaking belong to one another. At the end of this path, which is also the path of Greek as a language, the verb "is" becomes a subject, in the form of a substantival participle, "Being," describable and representable, round like a ball. It is at this very moment when Being acquires its name, *to eon*, and its self-identity that it, exactly like Odysseus, "motionless within the limits of mighty bonds," "abides firm where it is."[13]

Odysseus, then, planted there, sails by the Sirens and returns, after many trials and tribulations, to Ithaca. He is first recognized by his son, Telemachus, who sees him in the hut of the swineherd Eumaeus. Telemachus sees him first as an old man, covered in rags, and then as a god, after Athena has poured *kharis*, grace, upon his head. Perception alternates between the one and the other. Telemachus says to him: "For even now you were an old man in unseemly clothing, but now you resemble one of the gods who hold wide heaven" (XVI, 199–200, always this immanence . . .). Odysseus answers: "No other Odysseus than I will ever come back to you" (XVI, 204–205). The first recognition comes, therefore, from his son, a son's recognition that alternates between not enough and too much.

The only direct and immediate recognition comes from his dog, Argos, lice-ridden, lying on a heap of dung. He raises his head and pricks up his ears, for he "perceived that Odysseus had come close to him [*enoēsen Odussea*]" (XVII, 301). "Perceived" here translates *noein*, the same verb used to designate divine intuition, *noēsis noēsos* ("thought of thought"), in Aristotle's *Metaphysics*. Thus flair, *schnouf*, smell, also becomes a concept. Argos falls dead on his heap of dung.

And then comes the recognition by the nurse, who, while washing Odysseus's feet, sees and recognizes the scar left by a boar's tusk. We have here all the elements of tragedy: "recognition" (the *anagnōrisis* of Aristotle's

Poetics) based on a "mark" or "sign" (*sēma*), which can be found all the way up to Voltaire and in my mother's cross and embroidered clothes.

There remains one last recognition, but it is the one that counts, that of Penelope, his wife.[14] This recognition between husband and wife constitutes all by itself a whole odyssey of recognition. It is here that we can understand what "rootedness" truly means. Once again, at issue is a mark, the clasp of a cloak that is very "recognizable" but of no use because it comes too soon since Odysseus is still disguising the truth. Odysseus, says Odysseus, gave it to him: he thus begins by lying, as usual, by presenting himself as someone else. He persuades Penelope that he is not Odysseus but that he had once met him ("He knew how to say so many false things that were like true sayings" [XIX, 204]). She tells him she has dreamt of Odysseus, who assured her in her dream that he will be the eagle that kills the geese, the suitors, and that this is "no dream, but a blessing real as day [*ouk' onar all' hupar*]" (XIX, 547). They go to bed as strangers. She cries and dreams once again that Odysseus is sleeping by her side and that it is not a dream but reality (XX, 90).

The scene of the bow. Odysseus kills all the suitors with the help of Telemachus and two faithful companions, and he hangs the treacherous attendants. I gloss over these scenes of sound and fury. Finally he can appear before everyone's eyes as "Odysseus." Everyone's, but not yet Penelope's, for they are both still caught in the folds of the real, in ruses.

The faithful maidservants kiss him; the nurse awakens Penelope, whom Athena had put to sleep: "Odysseus is here, he is in the house, though late in his coming" (XXIII, 7). "Odysseus is here, he is in the house, just as I tell you. He is that stranger-guest . . ." (XXIII, 26–27). The circumspect Penelope tells the nurse that she is mad. Yet she believes her, leaps out of bed, cries with joy, but concludes in spite of everything that "Odysseus has lost his homecoming and lost his life, far from Achaia" (XXIII, 68). Nothing is more difficult than this misrecognition. She sits in front of him, eyes downcast, as women sometimes will, and she does not recognize him, or rather, she says nothing, her heart filled with "wonderment," like a tomb, "amazed" without being able to question him or look him in the eye.

Telemachus becomes indignant: "mother," "harsh mother with the hard heart inside you" (XXIII, 97). It's him and it's not him, in rags, some twenty years later, Odysseus, "if he is truly Odysseus, and he has come home" (XXIII, 107–108).

"Great-hearted Odysseus [is] in his own house" (XXIII, 153). He gives his orders full of ruse in order to prevent the dreadful consequences of the massacre and the families' vengeance. Then he takes a bath, is anointed with oil, puts on a mantle and a tunic, and grace covers his shoulders. He comes out of his bath looking like an immortal and takes up his seat. She of the "harsh heart," the "heart of iron," says nothing.

ROOTEDNESS IN THE PROPER SENSE

Penelope's recognition of Odysseus and, thus, of his identity, of he who is finally back home with his faithful wife, is linked to another sign of recognition that explodes the metaphor and describes "rootedness" properly speaking. Here is the passage in its entirety:

> Now the housekeeper Eurynome bathed great-hearted Odysseus in his
> own house, and anointed him with olive oil, and threw a beautiful
> mantle and a tunic about him; and over his head Athena suffused great
> beauty. . . . Then, looking like an immortal, he strode forth from the
> bath and came back then and sat on the chair from which he had risen,
> opposite his wife, and now he spoke to her, saying: "You are so
> strange. The gods, who have their homes on Olympus, have made
> your heart more stubborn than for the rest of womankind. . . . Come
> then, nurse, make me up a bed, so that I can use it here; for this
> woman has a heart of iron within her." Circumspect Penelope said to
> him in answer: "You are so strange. I am not being proud, nor indif-
> ferent, nor puzzled beyond need, but I know very well what you looked
> like when you went in the ship with the sweeping oars, from Ithaca.
> Come then, Eurykleia, and make up a firm bed for him outside the
> well-fashioned chamber: that very bed that he himself built. Put the
> firm bed here outside for him, and cover it over with fleeces and blan-
> kets, and with shining coverlets."

So she spoke to her husband, trying him out, but Odysseus spoke in anger to his virtuous-minded lady: "What you have said, dear lady, has hurt my heart deeply. What man has put my bed in another place? But it would be difficult for even a very expert one, unless a god, coming to help in person. . . . There is one particular feature in the bed's construction. I myself, no other man, made it. There was the bole of an olive tree with long leaves growing strongly in the court-yard, and it was thick, like a column. I laid down my chamber around this, and built it, until I finished it, with close-set stones, and roofed it well over, and added the compacted doors, fitting closely together. Then I cut away the foliage of the long-leaved olive tree, and trimmed the trunk from the roots up, planing it with a brazen adze, well and expertly, and trued it straight to a chalk line, making a bed post of it. . . . I lashed it with thongs of oxide, dyed bright with pur-ple. There is its character, as I tell you; but I do not know now, dear lady, whether my bed is still in place, rooted there [*empedon*], or if some man has cut underneath the stump of the olive, and moved it elsewhere." (XXIII, 153–204)

"Rooted there," solidly in the ground, *empedon*, like Odysseus before the Sirens and like Parmenides' Being. Far from being a metaphor, rootedness is first of all the rootedness of the nuptial and conjugal bed that is carved out of the trunk of the tree. One makes one's bed, now one must lie in it, a bed rooted for good in the ground of the home. And that is how you know you are at home. Penelope's heart and knees relax from the tension; she has recognized the "signs" (*sēmata*), signs of recognition that are themselves "well rooted" (*empeda*), like the bed in the olive tree, signs that proved it was Odysseus. Penelope weeps, rushes toward him and throws her arms around his neck, her tears pouring forth upon his face as she says, "Do not be angry with me, Odysseus, since, beyond other men, you have the most understanding" (XXIII, 209ff.).

Twenty years later, she too, his companion endowed with strategic intelligence (*periphrōn*: she perceives and thinks from all sides), needed to put her husband to the test (XXIII, 173), a revenge born out of wisdom and distance. For he never stopped lying to her and making her wait, he who passed himself off for another for the time he needed to avenge himself in safety, he who initially did not trust her, who had enough willpower to spend the first night of his return far from her, who did not rush to take her in his arms when he saw her cry, dream, feel that it was he. She will thus have shared mistrust with him, reticence, and ruse, at the same time as the sign-symbol of rootedness.

Love is *empedon*; it immobilizes. Odysseus complains of this when he is with Calypso: "There seven years I remained fastrooted [*empedon*]" (VII, 259). *Empedon* also describes the action of the net with which Hephaestus, having been cuckolded, ensnares Ares and Aphrodite: he "hammered out fastenings that could not be slipped or broken, to hold them fixed in position [*empedon authi menoien*]" (VIII, 275). But the "rootedness" is first of all, and this time without metaphor, that of the conjugal bed that weds nature and culture, the planted olive tree and Odysseus's *tekhnē*, his ingenious art and know-how as the master of the home. It is this coming together of nature and culture that makes one's home recognizable. "Rootedness": a properly nostalgic metaphor that is to be counted among all the other proper metaphors that the Odyssean *muthos*, myth and narrative, has transformed into a concept, for better and for worse.

What follows is the most tender part, the part that bespeaks the reciprocity of love: while it is Odysseus, the shipwrecked, who returns home, it is the sight of him that, for Penelope, is as sweet as the land is sweet for those who have been shipwrecked—and so, welcoming, she is welcomed. Her white arms cannot let go of his neck.[15]

The Shovel and the Oar

TIME IN UPHEAVAL: HOLD BACK THE NIGHT

Strange things happen with time at this point in time.

Odysseus never ceases to return. "Happy is he who, like Odysseus, can reach home . . . can return home, after a beautiful journey, full of hard-earned wisdom, to live with his kin for the rest of his life."[16] Nothing is less Homeric than Du Bellay's regret. First of all, Odysseus's journey is not, or not only, a beautiful journey; what is more, as soon as the hero returns, he must leave again just as soon, and that is the part that is often ignored or forgotten. The *Odyssey* is not over, or rather, the poem is over but not the journey. When Odysseus comes home, he has not yet returned, and he knows it. Before entering the bedroom and going to bed, he tells his newly refound companion that another trial awaits him: he must leave the next day to go even further, to the far reaches of a foreign land, as Tiresias has told him in Hades.

But before the next day, there comes that night, the first effect of the "not yet," a complicit dilation of time: Athena stops the Dawn at the edge of the Ocean; she prevents her from harnessing her two horses, Flamboyant and Shining; she prolongs the night covering the world. Out of pity, the gods hold back the night for the lovers. They rejoice in a loving embrace; they take pleasure in stories and exchange words before sleep falls upon them (XXIII, 300–301). The infinite is here in the finite, a perfect description of love.

One moment suffices, one moment to make an eternity—and simply to make the pain go away. A clinical question torments Bolzinger, who becomes the spokesperson for the doctor taking care of the Swiss: "how can a brief return-trip for a family embrace be a salvation for the one whose shaken morale led to the threshold of death? The effectiveness of the treatment by means of return, certified by two hundred years of medical practice, has never been analyzed in its principle."[17] And he goes on to cite the cases of soldiers for whom just seeing their village from afar, from a neighboring hill, or just seeing cows in a field, is all they need. A moment outside of time, a *kairos* that stands out in time, a rupture and an exception. There is surely nothing else that can compete with the "all" of time and the length of time that is lacking. Theology will have always known this: the moment/eternity.

WHERE IS (THE) ELSEWHERE?

> Eurynome, as mistress of the chamber, guided them on their way to
> the bed, and her hands held the torch for them. When she had brought
> them to the chamber she went back. They then gladly went together

to bed, and their old ritual [*hoi men epeita aspasioi lektroio palaiou thesmon hikonto*]. (XXIII, 293–296)

This is the end of the *Odyssey*, its accomplishment—the *telos Oduseias*, according to the old critical tradition. That is how the poem the *Odyssey* ends, but that is not how the return trip that is the Odyssey ends. With the news of the new departure, the long *Odyssey* we know comes to an end, but the other Odyssey, much lengthier, has barely begun. Odysseus returning has not yet returned, and this "not yet" is, to my eyes, precisely the time of nostalgia.

Not yet, but until when?

For Odysseus to be able to stay there, finally to be *there*, he must bring to completion a *ponos*, an arduous, onerous task, the fatigue that comes from another type of battle than that of arms, "unmeasured labor . . . both difficult and great" (XXIII, 250). The nature of this ordeal, in its very letter, holds an extraordinary symbolic force and is no more metaphorical than its earlier equivalent, the rooted bed.

It is in Hades, far from the light of the sun, amid lifeless shadows, that Odysseus, after having drunk the black blood, is told by the seer that he must go from city to city, carrying in his arms a polished oar, until he reaches a people who do not know the sea, or salted foods, or red-cheeked ships, or oars, which are a ship's wings.[18] The sign, easily recognizable, will be, says Odysseus, "when, as I walk, some other wayfarer happens to meet me, and says: what winnowing fan is that upon your shoulder?" (XXIII, 273–275).

He must thus take off again for the other end of the world, as far as possible from the Odyssey and the Mediterranean, all the way to the land of those who do not know the sea or Greek glory and who can confuse an oar for a winnowing fan, thus assimilating what they do not know to and through their culture, "integrating," we might say today, foreignness and alterity. I find this sentence mistaking the oar for a winnowing fan to be magnificent—"what winnowing fan is that on your shoulder?"—for it expresses in absolute misunderstanding but with absolute gentleness the farthest of the far. The misunderstanding that constitutes the relation between the proper and the foreign—this oar/this winnowing fan—is precisely the mark, the sure sign, of the elsewhere. Two complementary lessons: one cannot understand alterity without reducing it to the identical, and one cannot be certain about the elsewhere without recognizing this loss that produces assimilation.

Only on that day, then, will Odysseus have to "plant [his] well-shaped oar in the ground" (XIII, 276) and offer to King Poseidon the beautiful sacrifice of a bull, a ram, and a sow-mounting boar-pig. Poseidon, god of the Sea and father of the Cyclops whom Odysseus had blinded and defied, will no longer pursue him in hatred. Far inland, in the heart of the continent and not on the shores of islands, as far as possible from the sea. But then there is the sea, planted deep down in this land, stuck down inside and inscribed within it. Poseidon reigns at the farthest reaches, honored in a place where even his name is unknown. We can understand his satisfaction with the situation.

Only then will Odysseus be able to return home (*oikade*) (XXIII, 279). He will offer to the immortals a series of hecatombs, and then, he says: "Death will come to me from the sea, *ex halos*, in some altogether unwarlike way, and it will end me in the ebbing time of a sleek old age. My people about me will prosper" (XXIII, 281–284). To live, finally, "with [his] kin for the rest of [his] life," to die at home, at any rate. But the Greek itself, in its letter, is ambiguous precisely in this place: *ex halos*. Does this mean a death "outside the sea," without any meddling on the part of the sea, far from all shipwrecks? Or else (and this is the French translator Bérard's choice),[19] a death "come from the sea," gentle because that is where it comes from? This has been an issue for the critics, and they have been divided on it from the very beginning.

We too can set out again from there. At home, *oikade*, the sea of wandering yields to the earth where the bed is rooted. But as for this Odyssey after the *Odyssey*, the one that is to lead "elsewhere," we cannot even fathom how long it will take. Will there ever be an elsewhere radical enough, far enough, other enough, that an oar, if not that of a trireme then at least that of a rowboat on a river, will never have been seen or imagined? "A ship's wings": but who doesn't see birds, and who doesn't see water? The "not yet" can be indefinitely prolonged, and for the sake of pleasure. Isn't this something we all know?

For what, in the end, is nostalgia nostalgic? Nostalgia for the same, or nostalgia for the other? If it was sometimes enough for the Swiss just to see their village or a cow from afar in order to go away happy, it is probably because nostalgia has two sides: rootedness and wandering. Zimmermann, Haller's favorite pupil in Göttingen, the one who wrote the entry "nostalgia" in the supplement to Diderot and d'Alembert's *Encyclopedia* (the previous edition simply had an entry on *Hemvé* by Abbot Dubos), refused Catherine of Russia's offer to go to Russia so as to remain at home in Brugg. Yet he there experiences something like a nostalgia for elsewhere, as he writes in his *Treaty of Experience*: "Like me, every Swiss person experiences homesickness under a different name, from within his homeland, when he thinks he will live better abroad."[20] Let us then coin for him the term "planalgia," from *planē*, "wandering," *planaomai*, "to wander," like a "planet," this other word characteristic of the *Odyssey*, the one that characterizes this other aspect of Odysseus at sea, and mortals in general as Parmenides sees them,[21] the painful desire not to return but to wander—in common parlance, a need for fresh air and a desire to get away . . . But when Zimmermann decides to leave for the court of England, far from his village, where his learning is being stifled, he very quickly dies of nostalgia, as do his wife and daughter, who accompany him. The German language says it well: *Heimweh*, "homesickness," and *Fernweh*, "farsickness, longing for what is far away." Charybdis and Scylla.

It is probably Dante, read so carefully by the medievalist Ruedi Imbach, who best understood this other Odysseus. Imbach first refers to Levinas, for whom Odysseus is the symbol of a metaphysics of the Same whose essence is to return to the origin. That is why, Levinas says: "to the myth of Odysseus returning to Ithaca, we wish to oppose the story of Abraham who leaves his homeland forever for a yet unknown land, and forbids his servant to even bring back his son to the point of departure."[22] Either nostalgia or the promised land—though let's forget for the moment the nostalgia *for* the promised land. In Dante, Odysseus is in the Inferno. Whereas Odysseus is, for the Neoplatonists, the image of the soul that returns to its origin, "Dante inverts this symbolism: *Odysseus is an emigrant who no longer wishes to return.*" He thus becomes "the symbol of a knowledge that seeks only to seek and to explore" without any limits, beyond the pillars of Hercules.[23] Dante thus places him in the Inferno because, unlike Aeneas, he does not respect the limits of human reason in order to make room for faith, which is why he has to be shipwrecked. For those, however, who do not believe that room should necessarily be made for faith, the Odysseus who sets out again for an improbable and radical elsewhere, the emigrant who no longer desires to return, looks more like Odysseus than the Odysseus who has returned to his palace, a wise king, a good father and spouse. Odysseus *polutropos*, the one who is constantly inventing his life with one more ruse, cannot so easily become a househusband, cannot so easily find his place in one place.

When, then, are we ever at home? When is Odysseus ever at home? When he is *oikoi*, in his home? Three days: time to kill the suitors and unfaithful servants, time to be recognized by Telemachus, by the dog Argos, by the swineherd Eumaeus, by the nurse Eurykleia, by the good servants, by Penelope, by Laertes—by all those in Ithaca? Time to spend a long night with Penelope? Such a brief lapse of time compared to the wandering: three days at home in twenty years.

Or else, when he takes to the road again, until . . . Until he arrives at a place where what he is, where what determines him for better or for worse, the sea and its tempests, its sirens and its shipwrecks, its skiffs and its islands, is radically unknown? But wouldn't that mean that he is more at home everywhere else than in this improbable elsewhere? Home, then, is the Mediterranean. His identity, his "him" and "his home" [*son "lui" et son "chez lui"*], now extends to the limits of the known world.

Double Nostalgia

We could describe the internal tension proper to nostalgia in a different way: by using the two German words *Heimweh* and *Sehnsucht* as two representations of philosophy that the entire history of philosophy has never ceased meditating upon.[24]

On the one hand: *Heimweh* would be the desire to return, a closed-off nostalgia, one that goes round in a circle, like Giorgio de Chirico's Ulysses/Odysseus, who rows around his room in a pool of water, *home sweet home*— a wonderful painting from 1968. The room, no doubt a hotel room, is furnished with a large black wardrobe, a wing chair, and a kitchen chair. On the wall there is a de Chirico painting with a statue, and across the way a pane of glass, as opposed to a window, that looks onto a Greek temple. The sea in the middle of the room is a thick blue rug with curly edges, and a young Odysseus, alone in some kind of boat, is rowing assiduously. But the door is open!—a privileging of the cycle, of the circle, *kronos* as circular time.

Just a few remarks about this notion of time. This circular conception of philosophy, of philosophy as "re," is first of all modulated by a happy return toward the origin for Neoplatonism and its Christianizing interpretation of the *Odyssey*, with Odysseus, bound to the mast like Christ on the cross, a figure of the soul.[25] In modern times, it can be found in the reflexive taking up of circles within a circle by Hegel's owl of Minerva as well as in the Nietzschean transmutation, via the will to power, in the eternal return of the same. Odysseus, "through all his peregrinations, is only on the way to his native land"[26]: Odysseus's ideal is Penelope, the image of sedentary faithfulness, who weaves and unweaves in order to ensure the same but better.

On the other hand: *Sehnsucht* would be an open nostalgia that never "re"-turns to itself; it would be the indefinite infinite of the linear *aiōn*, a nonidentifiable, nonmathematizable infinite that flows but never stops. Philosophy as desire, as romantic as it is Lacanian, would then pursue an indeterminate object or an unfindable ideal: for Fichte, *das Sehnen* names "an aspiration (*Sehnen*) of the I; a tendency (*Trieb*) toward something absolutely unknown, which manifests itself only as a need (*Bedürfnis*), a disquiet (*Unbehagen*), a void (*Leere*) that seeks to fulfill itself and does not indicate what would allow this fulfillment."[27] From there, we can weave our way all the way to Lacan, to his unfindable and omnipresent "object *a*," the cause of desire. Odysseus the adventurer, the nomad, citizen of the world, all the way to the ends of the world, at home everywhere and nowhere.

This opposition is probably too simple to be maintained in the complexity of life or philosophy. Like the wave and the particle, they are two ways of seeing that go back and forth from one to the other. Each philosopher, each traveler, seeks to have his own way of seeing win out. With Odysseus, in any case, there are models aplenty, and all the interpretations-reinterpretations are valid, from the medieval Christians to Dante, from the Stoics to Horkheimer and Adorno.[28] He is at once the cosmopolitan hero and the bourgeois individual in search of his identity. Two Odysseuses in one, or, rather, a doubly vigilant nostalgia, as Günther Anders describes it: "When Odysseus was staying with Calypso, he had to be twice as vigilant. He not only had to be mindful to keep Ithaca in his heart but also not to lose the vision of his wanderings."[29] Nostalgia too is full of ruses, polytropic, with a thousand tricks up its sleeve.

Aeneas: From Nostalgia to Exile

"Make them all Latins with one language."

—VIRGIL, *The Aeneid* (VII, 837)

To Carry One's Homeland on One's Back

THE NOSTALGIA FOR THE FUTURE: REREADING AND REBINDING

Rootedness and uprootedness: nostalgia revolves around this.

When uprootedness occurs without any hope of return, the central figure becomes the one who has been exiled. Odysseus becomes Aeneas, the one the Greeks have thrown out of a Troy in flames and whose wanderings Virgil rather than Homer describes. And when the desire to return does not exist or exists no longer (for everyone knows that, fate or no fate, it is better to change one's desires than the order of the world), this figure becomes that of the emigrant who takes root in a different way—or, maybe, takes something other than root . . .

From nostalgia to exile, from one epic to another, the goal (*telos*) is no longer return and the home (*oikade*) but a founding, that of Rome, the

Rome of Augustus. The *Aeneid* is the tale of a long journey, parsed with the love stories and setbacks of the Trojan Aeneas on his way to Latium, where he will found a city, Lavinium, without which Rome cannot be conceived. Yet Rome is already there when Virgil is writing, not only founded but powerful, so that time is not a past pointing to the future through a poly-tropic present but something like a future anterior. Of course, the memory of the past remains present right up to the last breath, as we can hear in this famous and so very tender line of the *Aeneid*: *Et dulcis moriens reminiscitur Argos* (X, 782),[1] which, it seems, was cited in many medical theses written about nostalgia.[2] He looks up at the sky "and dies, remembering sweet Argos" (X, 782); that is how Virgil describes the death of Antores, Hercu-les' companion, who left Argos in order to join Evander in Italy and who is killed by a spear meant for Aeneas. But a strange memory of the future appears at the same time: nostalgia for the past, for a Troy destroyed and present in memory, comes to be associated with a nostalgia for Rome—for a to-come that is already there. Nostalgia is thus written in the future ante-rior, and that is no doubt the time of all foundings, which are perhaps only ever re-foundings. It is a matter, in short, of the retrospective power of truth, which constructs history via the narrative one gives of it, *history* and *story* [English in the original], as a performative of the past, for historians make a certain past exist when they write history, based on their knowledge of the present and according to their perspectives and their aims.

Ex-silio, or *exilio*, is *ex-salto*, to leap up into the air, to spring out of, to exult or jump for joy, but *exsilium* or *exsulium* is exile, banishment; one is *exsul patriae*, proscribed from one's homeland, *exsul mentis*, deprived of reason, and the etymology refers to *ex-solum*, to what is *hors-sol*, outside or removed from the land.

Removed from the land, going from land to land without being able to settle down, that is how Virgil describes Aeneas. From the *Odyssey* to the *Aeneid*, we are changing "keywords," to use the language of search engines and assessments. Wandering and return for the one (*Odyssey* I, 1–2, 9), fleeing and exile for the other (*Aeneid* I, 1–2; II, 639). Unlike Odysseus, who leaves his wife and son, his mother and father, back on his island, Aeneas flees carrying his homeland, his fatherland, on his back. In the literal sense: on the night of the fall of Troy, when there is nothing left to hope for, he spreads over his wide shoulders and bent neck the skin of a tawny lion, and he lifts up his father Anchises, asking him to take in his hands "sacred objects and household gods and relics" (II, 720–723, 717). His little boy, Iulus, follows him; his wife loses her way and dies.

We see here a new type of paganism: piety. Odysseus is *dios Odusseus*, "the divine Odysseus," in the adventurous permeability of the beauty of the world. Aeneas is *pius Aeneas*, "the pious Aeneas," bound to the homeland through the bonds of piety and religion. *Pietas* is the Roman virtue par excellence; it is, says Cicero, what "warns us to keep our obligations to our country or parents or other kin": the homeland, parents, gods.[3] As for *religio*, there are two competing etymologies, each as revealing as the other: *relegere*, from *legere*, "to collect, gather," and even "reread"—a way of contrasting an established observance that combines the practice of a ritual and its comprehension with various forms of superstition—that's the etymology given by Cicero,[4] and then *religere*, from *ligare*, according to Lactantius and Tertullian, which speaks of the bond of piety, both juridical and moral, by which we are "attached" to the gods and to the world that forms us. Aeneas is indeed an observer of bonds, bound every which way, and only this piety enables him to bind [*relier*] Troy to Rome and to reread [*relire*] Troy so as to found Rome.

The only thing that becomes certain over the course of the long exile is that there must not be a second Troy: it is not a matter of reproducing something in an identical way but of fabricating something else. Aeneas's exile is even punctuated by failed avatars of Troy that force him to continue on his way. In Thrace, Aeneas wishes to found "Aenead," after his name, but the trees begin to bleed.[5] They must pick up and leave. In Crete, he founds Pergamon, which is almost Troy's name (III, 133), but the plague strikes, and the Penates appear and order him to continue toward the Hesperides, that is to say, toward Italy. In Chaonia, Aeneas comes across a pseudo-Troy, founded by Andromache, abandoned by Pyrrhus, Achilles' son, and given to Priam's son Helenus, "Helenus, who named the fields Chaonian, calling the region Chaonia after Trojan Chaon, and built a Pergamum and Trojan citadel."[6] But this combination, which had everything going for it, is just a ludicrous replica: "As I advanced, I saw a little 'Troy,' and a replica of 'Pergamum' and a little river called the 'Xanthus,' and I embraced the portals of the 'Scaean Gates'" (III, 349–352).

Seven years after the fall of Troy—already a long time to wander—the winds take Aeneas back to Sicily, to the home of Acestes, the very place where Anchises had died a year earlier. Aeneas organizes celebratory games in commemoration of his father, but the Trojan women are at the end of their rope: "They long for a city; one and all they are sick of the sea" (V, 617); "over the ocean we pursue a fleeing Italy and toss on the waves."[7] Out of despair and exhaustion, they set fire to the boats. *Miserae ciues,* "unhappy women" (V, 671), Aeneas cries out. With some divine help, he asks Acestes to let them found a city in order to leave behind the women and old men, all of them tired of the sea. He marks out the boundaries with a plow, "assigning houses by lot, here Ilium and here Troy,"[8] but he names the city Acesta. There will never be a second Troy, only an Acesta for the exhausted Trojan women. Only *without* the women of old can the exile be transformed into immigration, into refoundation through cross-breeding. Aeneas thus once again departs, leaving all the women behind. Epics are written from one woman to the next: Odysseus leaves or refuses them (Calypso, Nausicaa) in order to find his own; Aeneas leaves or lets them kill themselves (Dido) in order to find the one he needs and does not yet know.

Everything is chiasmatic in the very letter of these texts and tales, a wholly motivated inversion.[9] Just as it is not a matter of recreating Troy, so it is not a question of reproducing the *Iliad* and the *Odyssey.* They must be reinvented through and through. It so happens that this type of "imitation" is called, precisely, culture. Juno's jealousy instead of Poseidon's anger, Venus's protection instead of Athena's, Jupiter's impartiality in place of Zeus's grand design, and, rather than Odysseus's tears when he hears the bard singing of his misfortunes during the Phaeacians' banquet, Aeneas's tears when he sees the war and his own silhouette on the bas-relief of Juno's temple in the sacred woods of Carthage. "A lifeless image," but one that transforms the glory of the Greek hero into a Roman monument—*kleos* into *monumentum.*[10]

RETURN TO THE SOURCE

The real difference is to be found, in the end, in the *telos* of the journey. While Odysseus at home has not really returned since he must leave just as soon for a radical elsewhere, Aeneas, when he reaches that unknown place, Italy, has returned to his origin: "I am Aeneas the Pious, and I carry in my vessels Penates snatched from the foe: my fame is known in Heaven. I seek my country, Italy, the cradle of my race" (I, 378–380).[11]

This forced and frenzied exile will have thus been, in its turn, only a way of returning home. The exile is a return to the origin, for the origin is not the one we thought it was. The Phrygian Penates, gods of fathers and of the homeland, dream with absolute precision:

> There is a land—the Greeks call it Hesperia—an ancient land, mighty
> in arms and rich in soil. Oenotrians inhabited it, but now men say
> that their descendants call it Italy, after their king. That will be our
> home, for Dardanus came from there and father Iasius, from whom
> the Trojans are descended. (III, 163–168)

It is, therefore, the Italian Dardanus who had to found the Dardanean Troy, the place from which Aeneas hails, Aeneas, whose exile now brings him back to his country of origin: Hesperia/Italy—the two points of view. Yet, it is as a stranger, as *externus*,[12] that Aeneas fulfills the oracle of Faunus, father of King Latinus, and as a stranger that he must be favored as son-in-law over Turnus, who is himself—I apologize for the complication— claimed by Amata, the wife of Latinus and the mother of the bride, to be *externus*, since he is king of an independent country and since his ancestors come from Mycenae.[13] The tale of the *Aeneid* is indeed hard to follow: we know it less well, and it duplicates the difficulties of the *Odyssey* by turning them inside out. But it is complicated for deep, violent, and decisive reasons, reasons that characterize the singularity and glory of Rome: inside-outside, it turns out that the exiled founder is a foreigner, but originally from here! Do we in fact ever really know where our neighbors come from? We got a hint of this when we spoke of Swiss nostalgia; the origin is used to this kind of ruse. The origin that claims to recount a clear and certain source and race never ceases to denounce itself as *a* point of view that is necessary for here and now, whether this be to establish an ideology or rectify one. When we read Herodotus, for example, we learn that the Pelasgians—in fact, the Athenian people were Pelasgians—spoke not Greek but a barbarian language, so much so that barbarity perhaps merits consideration. And when we read Denys of Halicarnassus, we learn that the Romans are a Greek colony, one that speaks a mixed language neither wholly barbarian nor completely Greek.[14] The origin allows one to win on both counts.

To Speak the Language of the Other

TO BECOME LATIN?

With the *Aeneid* and the founding of Rome, it is indeed a matter of language in the end.

Cano, says Virgil, and this "I sing of arms and a man" (I, 1), rather than *moi ennepe, Mousa*, "Tell me, Muse, of the man of many tricks" (I, 1) of the Odyssean prologue, means, as Florence Dupont so rightly suggests, "I am writing some Homer in Latin."[15] In order for Juno to leave Aeneas in peace, in order for her to allow this Trojan carrying his fatherland on his back to put an end to his wanderings, Jupiter must give in on one point, but it is an essential one: Aeneas will no longer speak Greek but Latin, the language of those who live where he is settling. Exile forces one to abandon one's mother tongue. Land of the fathers, language of the mothers: it is with the language of the other that one makes a new fatherland for oneself.

What becomes palpable in exile is the "*plus d'une langue*, that is, both more than a language and no more of *a* language." "*Plus d'une langue*": the quotation marks here indicate that this injunction-observation—for it is both at once—is a quote from Jacques Derrida. It is for him the very definition of what he calls "deconstruction."[16] The deconstruction by Jacques Derrida of his own position, rooted in his experience as a young *pied-noir* in Algeria, where Arabic was offered in schools only as an "optional foreign language," is expressed by an aporia, as banal as it is contradictory, which the title *The Monolingualism of the Other* already lets us hear.

> We only ever speak one language.
> We never speak only one language.[17]

From nostalgia to exile, from Odysseus to Aeneas, we go from the Greek language as *logos*, as universal tongue-language-reason, such as it is thought by those Greeks whom Momigliano qualifies (and this looks to my eyes like an epithet of nature) as "proudly monolingual,"[18] to the Latin language as second language, the language of those Romans who cannot not know that there are at least two languages. From *logos*, then, to languages and translation.

One can thus see the way in which politics or the political comes to complicate the universal. There are in fact two ways of being monolingual. The Greek way, which, if taken to its caricatural extreme, conceives of a monolingualism that is autochthonous (in the literal sense of being "born from the land"), with *logos* being the universal and unquestionable value from which is derived the strict opposition between Greek and Barbarian, an opposition so crude that it might well be barbarism itself. In Plato's *Menexenus*, Aspasia, who loves and advises Pericles, gives voices to this caricature. She there speaks words worthy of the National Front:[19]

> So firmly-rooted and so sound is the noble and liberal character of our city, and endowed also with such a hatred of the barbarian [*phusei misobarbaron*], because we are pure-blooded Greeks, unadulterated by barbarian stock. For there cohabit with us none of the type of Pelops, or Cadmus, or Aegyptus, or Danaus, and numerous others of the kind, who are naturally barbarians though nominally Greeks; but our people are pure Greeks and not a barbarian blend [*autoi Hellēnes ou mixobarba-roi*]; whence it comes that our city is imbued with a whole-hearted hatred of alien races [*katharon to misos . . . tēs allotrias phuseōs*].[20]

The Greeks themselves, Isocrates or Antiphon, for example, denounce this danger, but the danger remains.

The other way, the Latin way, is rooted in something like a politics of monolingualism that embraces an "inclusive alterity," to use Florence Dupont's expression, one that is open to cross-breeding.[21]

From this perspective, the key moment takes place right at the end of the *Aeneid* when Juno capitulates yet wins at the same time. Here is the exchange between the divine spouses:

> "Now for my part I yield, and leave the battle with loathing. This boon I beg—one which no law of Fate forbids, for Latium's sake and for the majesty of your kin: when they now make peace and a happy marriage (so be it!) and when they now are joined together in laws and treaties, *do not make the native Latins change their ancient name* [*nomen mutare Latinos*], nor become Trojans, nor be known Teucrians, *nor speak a different language* [*aut vocem mutare viros*], nor change their way of dress. Let Latium be—let Alban kings exist through the ages, let the Roman stock be strong, but with Italian valor. Troy has perished: let her name perish with her!" Smiling at her, the Creator of men and the universe said: "You are truly the sister of Jove, second child of Saturn: such great waves of anger surge deep in your breast! But come now, calm your anger that was begun in vain. I grant your wish, and freely give you what you ask: Italy's sons, the Ausonians,[22] *will keep their fathers' speech* [*sermonem Ausonii patrium*] and customs: their name shall be unchanged, the Trojans shall disappear, and mingle with the Latin race. Sacred laws and rites I shall add, and *make them all Latins with one language* [*faciamque omnis uno ore Latinos*]. From them will come a race of mixed Italian blood which you shall see surpassing man and gods in piety: nor shall any nation worship you so devoutly." Juno nodded assent and gladly changed her purpose. (XII, 818–841)[23]

The end of the exile, the moment of establishment-foundation, is a desired and happy cross-breeding: the Trojans who arrive will join bodies with the Ausonians, beginning with Aeneas and Lavinia. As always happens in politics, from the time of Alexander and his Diadochi all the way up to Napoleon and his marshals, the marriage of the exiled/conquering hero with the daughter of the leader seals the alliance. Cross-breeding is a—indeed *the*—condition for peace; the race is renewed, as if by an experienced breeder, and families are established. Language thus becomes the criterion for identity. Proper nouns first, the name of the people, the name of the place, all the eponymies that indicate belonging: "do not make the native Latins change their ancient name," begs Juno. "Their name shall be unchanged," responds Jupiter, smiling. Romulus, continuing the race of Aeneas, will found the city of Mars and call the people Romans after his own name—such has been Jupiter's grand design from the beginning (I, 254–296). Language itself is what is at stake: *Faciam uno ore Latinos*: "[I shall] make them all Latins with one language" (XII, 837), through a single language. Juno wins because the Greek language will no longer be the city's language; it disappears as a political language to the advantage of Latin, that of Virgil's *Aeneid* and Augustus's empire.

The poet knows just when to say that "Greece, the captive, made her savage victor captive": in this way, the Greek language becomes the language of culture for all Romans.[24] Yet—for there is no ambiguity here—it is Latin and Latin alone that unites Rome and that constitutes the Pax Romana. "Using Latin is for the Romans a sign of identity," writes Florence Dupont:[25] they impose it as another Greek language, "another language of civilization," the language of a new civilization.

"Included Alterity": We Are All Exiles

With Rome, homeland and origin no longer have quite the same meaning. The Romans impose their language, the language of "civil law" and of religion, but they do not identify with their language. In fact, "it does not bear their name; the Romans do not speak Roman." With Rome there is a transformation of the origin itself. Florence Dupont shows the importance of the strange ritual of *origo* on the Alban Mount, three public rites celebrated every year by the political elite of the city: the sacrifice to the Penates of Rome in Lavinium; the celebration of the Feriae Latinae, that is, the Latin Festival; and the renewal of the treaty that links Rome to Lavinium, this "ghost town" founded by Aeneas in the *Aeneid*. Such a juridical fiction is constitutive of Roman citizenship, and it becomes "the conceptual model for a Rome open to all foreigners," with Aeneas being the first among them. For Aeneas, this Italian Trojan, founds Lavinium, after his wife's name, but not Rome. Romulus will found the city only two generations later, after he has founded Alba. Hence the Romans who symbolically originate from Lavinium are also always already foreigners. With the awareness that the origin is a fiction—Lacan suggests writing "fixion," in order to show that it is a fabrication and not a given, a fiction that one chooses to fix—etymology replaces genealogy, and cross-breeding becomes the order of the day.

Rome thus becomes the paradigm of "included alterity"; any Roman citizen can have at least two homelands, one by nature, by his place of birth, the other by law, conferred upon him by *civitas*. Cicero says this very clearly through the words of Marcus: "all natives of Italian towns have two homelands, one by nature and the other by citizenship. Cato, for example, though born in Tusculum, received citizenship in Rome, and so, as he was a Tusculan by birth and a Roman by citizenship, had one homeland which was the place of his birth, and another by law."[26]

This does not prevent Rome, the *Urbs*, from being unique. It is by virtue of being a homeland for all, no matter where one is born, that it is unique, and it is this that makes exile, along with the nostalgia for Rome that accompanies it, a punishment worse than death. When Seneca was banished by Emperor Claudius *ad insulam*, to this wild Corsica—not far from "my home," in fact—he says this: "What more impoverished, if its resources be examined? What more uncivilized in terms of humans? What more forbidding in terms of the actual topography of the site? What more intemperate with regard to the nature of its climate?"[27] Consoling his mother, he consoles himself as the good Stoic he is, as free on the throne as he is in shackles, as Hegel says, always at home in his soul: "it is the soul that makes us rich; this is what accompanies us into exile, and in the most forbidding wilderness,"[28] so that we are all always at home wherever we are. But this demonstration meant to console also becomes historical and Roman, and it sends us back to Aeneas, the first exile: "Indeed, the very empire of Rome looks back for its founder to an exile, a refugee when his native city was captured, whom destiny brought to Italy, bringing with him his few remaining people and forced by fear of the conqueror to seek a distant country."[29] Migrations, immigrations, conquests—no part of humanity has remained in its place of origin—all "these are nothing other than public exiles":[30] we are all exiles!

It is Ovid, having been relegated by Emperor Augustus to the Scythians, at the outermost limits of the Black Sea, there where one awaits the barbarians, who underscores in a particularly poignant way everything that is at stake in language. Without his books, without Rome, it is as if civilization itself had been forbidden to him. He is afraid he will forget Latin:

> There isn't a book to be found, there's no one to read any poem to, nor is there a person at hand who can understand what I may say. The entire region is one of barbaric, animal voices; everywhere is filled with the sounds of fear and the clamor of war. I seem to myself to have lost the power to speak my own language for I have learned to speak Sarmantian and Getic instead.[31]

Nostalgia is here, more than ever, a desire to return to one's homeland, to where the gods, and the divine Caesar who represents and stands in for them—"divine" in a completely different sense than the "divine" Odysseus—have cast you out from in order to punish you, and only Caesar's forgiveness will allow you to see the day of return. It is as if there is nothing for you to learn elsewhere, since everything is there where you no longer are. All you can do is write some moving *Tristia* and send the book on ahead of you as your herald.[32]

Two unique languages, in short: the unforgettable Greek and the imperial Latin. Two types of hegemony: cultural and political. And then all the other languages, which are merely deemed *idiotes*, that is to say, apolitical and barbaric, deprived of culture, languages spoken at home, in their place of origin. Obviously, this would have to be the starting point, whether by way of comparison or contrast, for thinking about the linguistic politics of today, whether we are talking about the eleven national languages recognized in the constitution of South Africa, about the requirement of Hebrew for Israel, or of French in order to become French, or else about *globish*, *global English* [English in the original], the language of empire and/or the service language for everyone in today's globalized world.

The result of Aeneas's exile—the double origin of Rome, with at least two languages—complicates nostalgia all the more and forces us to construct the relationship between language and people in a different way. That is the place from which I would now like to set off anew.

Arendt: To Have One's Language
for a Homeland

The Europe of the pre-Hitler period? I can't say that I don't have any
nostalgia for it. What remains? The language remains.

—HANNAH ARENDT[1]

The Language and the People

ASSIGNING IDENTITY: A POLITICAL PREDICATE
AND NOT AN ESSENCE

Aeneas will no longer speak Greek but Latin. The sign of exile is the transformation in one's relation to language: exile denaturalizes the mother
tongue. Aeneas no longer speaks the *logos*, like Odysseus, but one language
among others. And when one settles down in another "homeland," one
becomes "naturalized." Hannah Arendt lived and thematized this relation
to language, to culture, and to the homeland of her childhood with the
greatest lucidity in a number of texts, letters, and interviews, during her
long exile, beginning with her flight from Germany in 1933, her stay in
France as a refugee, her arrival, by way of Lisbon, in the United States in
May 1941 with the status of stateless person, and her eventual "naturaliza-

tion" as an American citizen some ten years later, in 1951. Günter Gaus, in an interview for German television that was shown in 1964, asks her if she misses pre-Hitlerian Germany, the space-time of her birth. She responds: "The Europe of the pre-Hitler period? I can't say that I don't have any nostalgia for it. What remains? The language remains" ("LR" 12).

It is the mother tongue, not the land of her fathers, that constitutes her homeland: instead of agreeing to Latin in order to found Rome, it is the resistance of German in New York that makes the homeland. By the same token, Arendt teaches us how to detach language from people even more radically. The German language and the German people are not identical or superimposable in any way, especially not politically. It is another conception of the homeland that comes to light after the horrors of the war, one that is more Roman than Greek, or, according to a contemporary philosophical classification, more Arendtian than Heideggerian, and, without any doubt, politically relevant today.

The difference between the mother tongue and the land of the fathers is linked to the extreme caution that must accompany any assignation of identity and, above all, that of "Jewish" identity. We know from Odysseus that every odyssey amounts to putting into narrative form the assignation of identity. Arendt used to say that she did not know she was Jewish when she was a little girl. "I first met up with it through anti-Semitic remarks— they are not worth repeating—from children on the street" ("LR" 6). Indeed, I believe, from personal experience, that being Jewish, like being a woman, requires at the very least that you be told this, that it be made known to you. It is not a direct identity but a mirroring relation, a differential assignation. Arendt's level-headedness, which she gets from her mother, a Jewish mother obviously but also a socialist mother faithful to Rosa Luxemburg, can be summed up in a single sentence that becomes a kind of watchword for her: "if one is attacked as a Jew, one must defend oneself as a Jew" ("LR" 12).[2] As a Jew and a woman, I myself would say the same thing, and I recognize in it the level-headedness that is passed down from mother to daughter.

But it is important to understand, as Arendt herself points out, that this response is political, "purely political." There is no essentialization, no naturalization, no substance, just a simple predicate—and this is, to my eyes, what justifies the connection to "gender."[3] Here is the "as" so characteristic of philosophy, from Aristotle's "being as being" up to Heidegger by way of Kant, an "as" that changes meaning and becomes political. We understand, then, why Arendt resists being called "a philosopher" and, even more, a specialist in "political philosophy," an oxymoron from Plato to Heidegger.[4]

Such a way of thinking Jewish identity serves Hannah Arendt as a model for thinking her German identity. "I myself, for example, don't believe that I have ever considered myself a German—in the sense of belonging to a people as opposed to belonging to a state, if I may make that distinction" ("LR" 8). She did not feel herself to be German any more than Jewish, in the sense of belonging to the Jewish people: that's exactly what she was often criticized for, especially by Gershom Scholem. Scholem accuses her of not having enough love for the Jewish people in *Eichmann in Jerusalem*. He writes to her, "I regard you wholly as a daughter of our people, and in no other way" (*JW* 466). To which she responds:

> The truth is I have never pretended to be anything else or to be in any way other than I am, and I have never even felt tempted in that direction. It would have been like saying that I was a man and not a woman—that is to say, kind of insane. . . . To be a Jew, to be a woman, belongs for me to the indisputable facts of my life . . . what has been *given* and not *made* . . . *physei* and not *nomōi*. (*JW* 466)

But she then goes on to differentiate between love and politics in a very incisive manner: "You are quite right. . . . I have never in my life 'loved' any people or collective—neither the German people, nor the French, nor the American, nor the working class or anything of that sort. I indeed love 'only' my friends and the only kind of love I know of and believe in is the love of persons" (*JW* 466–467). And when Gaus mentions this testimony given about herself, Arendt forcefully corroborates it by differentiating between two types of belonging, which, precisely because they cannot be confused, are the condition for freedom. "Belonging to a group," she repeats, "is a natural condition. You belong to some sort of group when you are born, always." That is the place for love and friendship. But it is disastrous to mistake this with belonging to a group "in a second sense," an organized, political group with common interests in its relation to the world. Any talk of love is thus always "apolitical" and "worldless" ("LR" 17).

But then what about Jewish identity? As a predicate for a person, it is first and foremost a good way of putting subtraction to use. Neither denial nor negation, then—as with "those Jewish or non-Jewish antifascists who believe they are doing something to benefit the Jews by debating them out of existence" (*JW* 263)—but subtraction, which is exemplified by what Arendt calls "the conscious Pariah" (*JW* 283).[5] Like her, the pariah remains outside, outside any institution and outside *doxa*—like her and, first of all, like her mother, like and with her mother: it is a "standing outside of all social connections," she tells Gaus ("LR" 17). "Nonconformism is almost the *sine qua non* of intellectual achievement."[6] Elisabeth Young-Bruehl tells how Arendt would tear herself away from any situation of obedience by a *"This place ist nicht für meiner Mutter Tochter,"* a sort of carp's leap back toward the mother tongue ("this place"—in English—"is not for the daughter of my mother"—in German). Outside, therefore, even vis-à-vis the Jewish community and vis-à-vis Israel, each time it became necessary, that is, politically necessary.[7]

Her essence, then, if essence there is, is philosophy: "For me the question was somehow: I can either study philosophy or I can drown myself, so to speak" ("LR" 8). But a philosophy far from the "circle of philosophers," one that she will call, in her interview with Gaus, by a different name, that of "political theory."

PHILOSOPHY, POLITICS, AND MOTHER TONGUE: INVENTION AND CLICHÉ

What are exile and nostalgia for a philosopher of this kind? We are here approaching a definition of philosophy in its relation to language. Arendt is an exile less from her country, Germany, than from her language, German. She says so and repeats it with the utmost lucidity in her interview with Gaus. Let me underscore, once again, the sharp distinction she makes between mother tongue and fatherland, that "pre-Hitlerian Germany" that Günter Gaus asks her about. To the question of whether she misses it, she responds by extending the question to the whole of Europe: "The Europe of the pre-Hitler period? I can't say that I don't have any nostalgia for it. What remains? *The language remains.*" I have used as an exergue this sentence, which became the title of the interview: "What Remains? The Language Remains."[8] Arendt has just made it clear, as we have seen, that she has never "considered [herself] a German"—in the sense of belonging to a people as opposed to a state: neither a people nor a fatherland but merely a nationality, which has itself, in fact, changed. What always counts, what counts forever—*immer*, repeats Derrida—has nothing to do with any of this: language is what counts.[9] "There is a tremendous difference between your mother tongue and another language. For myself I can put it extremely simply. In German I know a rather large part of German poetry by heart; the poems are always somehow *in the back of my mind* [in English in the original]. I can never do that again" ("LR" 13).

This is her unshakable feeling, one that is sufficient to define exile, from the 1940s to the end of her life. She writes in 1943: "We refugees have lost our home, which means the familiarity of our daily life. We lost our occupation, which means the confidence that we are of some use in this world," but, above all, "we lost our mother tongue, which means the naturalness of reactions, the simplicity of gestures, the unaffected expression of feelings" ("WR" 264). Hannah saying "*Ach!*" ("This power of being seized [by an idea, an emotion, a presentiment] . . . often with a start, widened eyes '*Ach!*' . . . set her apart from the rest of us like a high electrical charge"[10]). Almost twenty-five years later, having been an American lecturer and professor for more than fifteen years, she repeats these sentiments: "You know I had to leave Germany more than thirty-four years ago; the mother tongue is the only thing you can take with you from the old country, and I have always tried to keep this irreplaceable thing intact and alive."[11]

That is how the situation becomes intolerable for the refugee who obeys and follows the good advice of his or her saviors (or, today, the requirements of the host country). And if it is not intolerable, that is a bad sign.

"We were told to forget; and we forgot quicker than anybody ever could imagine. . . . After four weeks in France or six weeks in America, we pretended to be Frenchmen or Americans," she writes in 1941 ("WR" 265). As refugees, we find it hard to forget our profession or our social status; "with the language, however, we find no difficulties: after a single year optimists are convinced they speak English as well as their mother tongue; and after two years they swear they speak English better than any other language—their German is a language they hardly remember." She comes back to this in her interview with Gaus: "I have always consciously refused to lose my mother tongue. I have always maintained a certain distance from French, which I then spoke very well, as well as from English, which I write today" ("LR" 12–13). One has to hear Hannah Arendt speak English "with a very heavy accent," expressing herself "unidiomatically," one has to translate the texts Arendt wrote in English to understand to what extent, from the sound to the syntax and rhythm of her writing, she cultivates (*colere*, a verb that can be used for the field, the soul, and the gods) only the German language. Günther Anders, her first husband, talks about the "stammering existence" of exiles who are tossed about "not only from country to country, but language to language"—"many of us became real stammerers—even in both languages." And it's probably with Hannah in mind that he speaks of those who, noticing the danger, "devoted themselves fanatically to the mother tongue . . . because language was the only thing that could not be taken away from them, the only part of their home they still mastered."[12]

But what is it that makes a tongue a "mother tongue"? Perhaps the possibility of invention. Poetry, this making (of) language, is naturally bound up with the mother tongue. Each speaker is an author in his or her language and of his or her language—"he or she is its organ and it is his or hers," as Schleiermacher rightly says[13]—so that, rather than using it as a static totality, one produces it as *energeia* and not as *ergon*, as putting into work, into act and evolution. Arendt underscores this: "I do things in German that I would never allow myself to do in English" ("LR" 13).

Holding on to one's mother tongue is not some coquettish resistance but a very deep fear, and it makes sense, it seems to me, only when it is seen in light of Arendt's conception of the banality of evil. With exiles who speak foreign languages much better than she can, "one cliché chases another" ("LR" 13). The productivity, inventiveness, and authority one displays in one's language come to be, she says, "cut off" the more one forgets. "Cliché" is the term we need to focus on here. The banality of evil—think of Eichmann, the specialist—is not without relation to the banality of the language one speaks. As Anders underscores: "we become the way we speak" (*JE* 106). The cliché must not be mistaken for an ordinary use of words, for ordinary language: on the contrary, each word of ordinary language is full of all the associations and meanings that have accrued to it, *in the back of the mind*.[14] Arendt speaks of "Eichmann's heroic fight with the *German language*, which invariably defeats him."[15] "He apologized, saying, 'Officialese [*Amtssprache*] is my only language.' But the point here is that officialese became his language because he was genuinely incapable of uttering *a single sentence that was not a cliché*" (*EJ* 48; my emphasis). Arendt speaks of Eichmann's "horrible gift for *consoling himself with clichés*" (*EJ* 55; my emphasis) in the context of the "reconciliation" he sought. Hence Eichmann said that he

> "would like to find peace with [his] former enemies"—a sentiment he shared not only with Himmler . . . but also, unbelievably, with many ordinary Germans, who were heard to express themselves in exactly the same terms at the end of the war. This *outrageous cliché* was no longer issued to them from above, it was a self-fabricated stock phrase, *as devoid of reality as those clichés by which the people had lived for twelve years*; and you could almost see what "an extraordinary sense of elation" it gave to the speaker the moment it popped out of his mouth. (*EJ* 53; my emphasis)

One can thus speak one's mother tongue using clichés: here is the proof! If invention is really something proper to oneself, like the "mother," then one would have to conclude, in all good logic, that one's tongue is no longer a "mother tongue" as soon as one no longer invents anything in it, indeed, that it is no longer even really a "tongue" for all those politically and humanly idiotic listener-transmitters crippled by banalities and lacking in any reflective or critical judgment. The German language will still be a mother tongue for exiles, but it was no longer one for ordinary Nazis: this is the result of the decoupling of language and people pushed to the extreme. For lack of a mother tongue, when the mother tongue is no longer a tongue, a language, there is only propaganda. In fact, it is because we have a responsibility with regard to the words we use, the responsibility of an author and not of a receiver or communicating go-between, that language is also something political. Arendt's entire perception of language is rooted in the Aristotelian definition of man as *zōion logon ekhon*, an animal endowed with language, "a political animal in a greater measure" than any other animal because he is endowed with language.[16] In a general way (and this is a theme characteristic of sophistics, of which there would be much to say), the political force stems from its performative effect. Arendt underscores this anti-Aristotelian, antiphenomenological, and antionto- logical orientation that no longer goes from being or thought to language but the reverse, from language to thought and to being: "All that for which language has a word exists for thought; all that for which language does not have a word escapes thought . . . . It is an error to think that a reality thought in language is less real than a lived reality that is not thought. As far as man is concerned, it might very well be the contrary."[17] The perfor- mative force inherent to language as political means that only an extreme vigilance can avoid an extreme error, for obedience and the banality of evil are conveyed incognito through clichés and through what we call today, with a terrible equanimity, "the elements of language."

The question that can no longer be avoided is thus that of the relation between propaganda, this lack of invention that rides on the back of a lack of taste—taste being the political faculty par excellence—and mass com- munication or indeed communication in general. Reading Arendt, I feel like saying that obedient refugees speak *globish*. It can happen that one speaks in clichés—that is the banality of evil—in one's maternal language. But how does one avoid speaking in clichés in a language that is not one's own? That is precisely Arendt's fear as she clings to her mother tongue. We are here touching upon the theme of the "crisis of culture." Mass culture, mass communication: when the language in general use is no longer anything but *globish*, that is, *global English*, and there is no longer any invention, taste, or judgment, then there is quite simply no longer any language. In fact, the British Council is so worried about this that it commissions one study after another to measure the loss within the English language of the very thing that makes a language a language.

HEIDEGGER'S NOSTALGIA, ARENDT'S NOSTALGIA

The mother tongue is unlike any other tongue not simply because it is the language or tongue of the mother—and one has only one mother—but because it constitutes one's very being through a complete imbrication of nature and culture. How can we "have" a language without "being" in the process constituted by this sonorous mix of signifiers and life, that is, without it having us? How can we think this privilege of the mother tongue without at the same time considering it superior to the others, as something of absolute genius? How can we avoid the cumbersome problem of the "genius" of languages? Aren't we taught language by our homeland, our country, our culture, our tradition—in short, by a whole people? As Protagoras already said, there is more than one nurse; from the *pedotribe* who teaches children to read to the legislator, they are all nurses.[18] With this thought of the absolute singularity of the mother tongue, we are all too quickly thrown back to the Greek *logos*, to a paradigm that constitutes a universal on the basis of a singular, to the point of being able to use the same word to say language, tongue, thought, style, intelligence, and intelligibility—*ratio et oratio*. The couple *Greeks/Barbarians* says this with a crudeness, a cruelty, that is almost without limits, and the verbs "Hellenize/barbarize" do so even more: the Greeks Hellenize. Just by reading Homer one learns to speak Greek, to speak well, to think correctly, to be cultured, to be civilized, in short, to be men, and one thereby differentiates oneself from "barbarians" (we would say "foreigners"), that is, from those we cannot understand, who do not speak Greek, who commit barbarisms in language, who are neither cultured nor civilized, who are not men like us, who are not men at all. . . . Isn't belonging to a people precisely this imbrication of language and culture? How, by what force, can one prevent this from turning into "nature"?

It is here that we need to follow very strictly Arendt's decoupling of language and people. One should thus say: one is not born German, one becomes German, and we would then be not unlike Isocrates, for whom it is the Greeks, those who think that *hellēnizein* ("being Greek," Hellenism) comes from nature and not culture, who are the real barbarians.[19] To have one's language for one's only homeland: we must come to understand exactly what this distance implies—in other words, we need to measure the impact of the "as a Jew."

The comparison with Heidegger, which, to my knowledge, Arendt herself never directly makes, sheds light on everything here. I always come back to this line of Heidegger's, which, through the thought of being, makes this confusion of language and people readable in a rather caricatural way:

> The Greek language is philosophical, i.e., not that Greek is loaded
> with philosophical terminology, but it philosophizes in its basic struc-
> ture and formation. The same applies to every genuine language, in
> different degrees to be sure. *The extent to which this is so depends on the
> depth and power of the people and of the race who speak the language and
> exist within it.* Only our German language has a deep and creative
> philosophical character comparable to Greek.[20]

For Heidegger, then, it is Greek, or rather German, more Greek than Greek, that is rooted in the German people: an "ontological nationalism," therefore, against the backdrop of German romanticism.[21]

That is how I would take account of what I suggest calling the disparity between the two nostalgias: Arendt, as a refugee and thinker of the political, is nostalgic for German and is exiled from one language among others; Heidegger, as a philosopher, is nostalgic for Being and is exiled from *logos*—better yet, from *die Sprache* ("Language," the "Said"), "the house of Being" and "the home of man's essence."[22] One would need to be more subtle here, or more philosophical, than I am or wish to be. We cannot reduce Heidegger's homeland to the nationalism of National Socialism, even if his wife Elfriede, his "dear little soul," is all too much the symbol and symptom of this kind of homeland. For we are dealing explicitly here with *Being*, for example in the "Letter on Humanism":

> This nearness "of" Being . . . from the experience of the oblivion of Being is called the "homeland." The word is thought here in an essential sense, not patriotically or nationalistically but in terms of the history of Being. The essence of the homeland, however, is also mentioned with the intention of thinking the homelessness of contemporary man from the essence of Being's history.[23]

In short, and with the *y* that is part of Heidegger's language in 1933–1935, "*das Vaterland ist das Seyn selbst* [The 'fatherland' is beyng itself]."[24] This is why nostalgia is said by Heidegger to be "the very determination of philosophy."[25] In his 1929–1930 course, he cites a line of Novalis according to which "philosophy is really nostalgia, an urge to be at home everywhere," and he then offers this comment: "philosophy can only be such an urge if we who philosophize are *not* at home everywhere"—*nicht zu Hause*, says Heidegger, in fact, "nowhere at home." "It is a strange, romantic, definition," he goes on to say: nostalgia, "*Heimweh*, homesickness—does such a thing still exist today at all?" "To be at home everywhere means to be at once and at all times *within the whole*. We name this '*within the whole*' and its character of wholeness the *world*." It is toward the world, toward "this within the whole," that we are "on the way," "driven in our nostalgia." We ourselves are this "underway," "this neither the one nor the other." It is "the unrest of this 'not,'" he adds, that "we name *finitude*." Thus: "Philosophy, metaphysics, is a nostalgia, an urge to be at home everywhere," everywhere because nowhere.

It is very notable that the place, the "site" of reference, is ontological (Being) and not political (the state, the city)—ontological *so as not* to be political, I would be tempted to say. The interpretation that Heidegger consistently gives of the first *stasimon* of Sophocles' *Antigone* is a striking testimony to this. Man is what is most *unheimlich*; he is "the strangest of all" (*to deinotaton*) because he is *hupsipolis apolis*. What does this mean? Heidegger here uses the Greek to go more deeply into the German, though also the German to go more deeply into the Greek. He chooses to hear in *polis* not "city" or "city-state," as it is traditionally translated—a "political" terminology, precisely—but, rather, and as always first, "being." *Polis* means, instead, "the historical place, the there *in* which, *out of* which, and *for* which history happens."[26] Heidegger will come back to this eight years later, by etymologizing fancifully in *Parmenides*: *polis* is "the pole"[27] of the *pelein*, *pelein* being the old Greek word for "to be." So much so that the man above the *polis* and without *polis* finds himself—unlike Oedipus, the wanderer, who is guided by his daughter, Antigone, and who is above the city outside the city—"eminent in the site of history" at the same time as he is "without city or site," "without institution or borders," since he must first of all "found" all of this. Of course, Being is commonly a less toxic word than ground, race, or rootedness, and Heidegger, as a philosopher, is here able to avoid speaking, as Barrès does, of the dead and of being rooted in the ground.

But is this German language, informed by the Greek, the one for which Arendt is nostalgic?

The Faltering Equivocity of the World

Of Languages as Exiled—and of German

Arendt often tells us how important the Greek language and Greek poetry were to her.[28] But the decoupling she suggests between language and people uproots, "de-races," we might say, language and prevents all slippage. If we endorse this Arendtian decoupling, then language can no longer be proper to a people; it is not a property. Jacques Derrida has said this with the greatest force: "I have only one language, and, at the same time, in an at once singular and exemplary fashion, this language does not belong to me. . . . A singular history has exacerbated in me this universal law: a language is not something that belongs."[29] Language is thus detached from a people so that it itself, language itself, may remain.

It is, I believe, the same gesture when we go from man—Man as *hupsipolis apolis*, the being from afar, the being-there of a Being that is itself not there—to men in their diversity and plurality: a single and same consideration of the multiple imposes the political as opposed to the ontological. From the universal or the generic to the particular—that is Arendt's constant concern: the concern for human plurality.

What is politics?

1. Politics is grounded in a fact: human plurality. God created *man*, *men* are a human product, terrestrial . . .
2. Politics has to do with the community and the being-together of beings who are *different*.[30]

She repeats this in English three months later: "If Man is the topic of philosophy and Men the subject of politics, then totalitarianism signifies a victory of 'philosophy' over politics—and not the other way round."[31] I have recently discovered that Günther Anders says this with perhaps even greater force than Arendt, inscribing a singular plurality at the center of the wholeness that each one of us is: "What I mean is that *man* is *men*; he exists only in the plural. . . . 'Men' is not the plural of the singular 'man'; each man is already a form of 'men' in the singular" (*JE* 236).[32] There is the same relationship (the same *logos*, the Greeks would in fact say) between Man and men as between the language of Being (the Heideggerian language of the *es gibt*, of the *there is* of the ontological giving) and one language among others (the "there is" of the plurality and diversity of languages, thought by Humboldt in particular),[33] even if, in both cases, the language in question goes by the name of German.

Let us start again. Which language are we talking about? For Arendt: the German language. And which people? For Arendt: no people / the Jewish people (according to the factual resonance of the "as," a response to Israel, to Auschwitz). In any case, there is never anything like "the language of my people." Hannah Arendt tried to learn Hebrew with a friend and colleague in New York. She made a great effort, but without changing her opinion: "Hebrew . . . is not a language but a national disaster!" she writes to Blücher in August 1936.[34] It so happens that Arendt's mother tongue is

the German language. "The German language is the essential thing that
has remained and that I have always consciously preserved." "Even in the
most bitter of times?" Gaus then asks, and Arendt responds: "Always. I
have said to myself: What am I to do? It wasn't the German language after
all that went mad. And, second, there is no substitution for the mother
tongue" ("LR" 114). This answer, the hypothesis of the madness of language, deeply moves Derrida. What exactly does language in its "genius"
and its "mother"-like individuality have to do with the language of the
German people in Nazi Germany? Is it or is it not above, outside, or beside
what took place "within" it, in German?

"How to speak after Auschwitz?": the question is well known. We know
all too well that it shapes at once the philosophical concerns of Adorno—
a visceral feeling of disgust for Heidegger's language, which must be both
singularized as jargon and generalized as a totalitarian language in order
to achieve the preservation of the German language—the carefully chis-
eled poetic silence of Celan, with fragments of language filtered through
the partition of a confessional, *Sprachgitter*, without the hope of any phoe-
nix, without any hope at all; and, finally, the irrefutable philological
insights of Victor Klemperer in *Lingua Tertii Imperii*, the title with which
he designates the language of the Third Reich. Klemperer was a professor
of French literature relieved of his chair at the University of Dresden. In
The Journal of a Philologist, which he writes from his "Jew house," keeping
time as if to keep his inner freedom ("I feel like Odysseus in Polyphemus's
cave: 'You I shall eat last'"[35]), he keeps careful, almost hourly note, from
1936 to 1945, of the way in which Nazism infuses and transforms the
German language. "Words can be like tiny doses of arsenic: they are swal-
lowed unnoticed, appear to have no effect, and then, after a little time, the
toxic reaction sets in after all." That is why, Klemperer adds, "many words
in common usage during the Nazi period should be committed to a mass
grave for a very long time, some forever."[36] We must throw away words,
the word *organize*, for example, throw away, without any shame and out in
the open, certain "elements of language," as we call them today, certain
uses of language. But what does "throwing a language away" mean?
Whence the perplexity of the exile who has finally returned home:

Anders, for example, who exclaims and wonders, "Here they speak German again! . . . The first instantaneous impression is surprise. 'Do you hear? They're speaking German.' But the second impression is that it is 'impudence.' Why?" And he goes on to add: "I fear that by going back to the old country, we, the poets of exile, have reduced our muse to silence" (*JE* 123, 127).

It is this question of the after-Auschwitz that Arendt seems to me to reinitiate or reinitialize. The German language has not gone mad, for the German language is not the German national language or the National Socialist language but a language unto itself, itself outside the land, not belonging, literally "exiled." It is because every language is, as language, outside the land, exiled, and not only exiled but spoken in exile (which in some ways proves its exiled character) that this question makes no sense. Denaturalizing the mother tongue—that, at the end of the day, is always what saves it.

The Paradigm of Translation

This is, it seems to me, what Derrida really understood and what he recalls with his injunction-exclamation: "(No) more than one language!"

That is why, for Arendt, love for the mother tongue, the fidelity owed to it by the exile in order to exempt it from having also been the language of Nazi Germany, is combined with and follows the plurality that she simultaneously practices and promotes. Indeed, she constantly experiences in a close and personal way the plurality of languages. That's how she writes her *Denketagebuch*, each time letting the object, whether it be Plato, Machiavelli, Pascal, or Kant, come in the language of the work, and even, on occasion, in a rather jubilatory and carefree manner, in the language she has at hand, for example a common English translation of Plato when she does not have the Greek text, even Kant in English, "and basta!"[37] Elisabeth Young-Bruehl speaks of the "originary languages of Arendt," "the language of her philosophical and poetic homeland, German, the language of her first exile, French, the language of her second citizenship, English-with-a-German-accent, and the languages of her political forebears, Latin and Greek."[38] Indeed Arendt has "more than one language," even in just her attentiveness to Latin as a counterpoint to Greek. That is already a great point of difference between her and Heidegger and the constellation *logos-Sprache-Sage*: thanks to Arendt, the Latin words *cultura, gravitas, auctoritas, religio, libertas,* and *traditio* have become the foundation of our politicophilosophical present.[39] I see here an essential difference with regard to the experience and paradigm of translation, since it is "in Latin" that Greek, for Heidegger, got lost philosophically, whereas, for Arendt, it got politically reinvented.

As a result, it is no longer so certain that invention is proper to the mother tongue. If it is necessary to know a language intimately in order to be able to invent within it, then there are perhaps different kinds of intimacy. The poet Randall Jarrell, born in Nashville, Tennessee, who worked at the *Nation* and, with Arendt, for the publisher Schocken Books, and who, according to her, excelled in "Englishing" her texts, deeply loved the German language:

> I believe
> —I do believe, I do believe—
> The country I like best of all is German.

And he would sigh "Alas, my German isn't a bit better: if I translate, how can I find time to learn German? If I don't translate, I forget about German."[40] That sometimes happens, doesn't it? It happens that one dreams or invents striking sentences in a language one does not speak very well; it's a way of declaring one's love for that language. If it is not easy to know what changes in us when one changes the language for us, it is also not easy to know what we change within us when we change languages, when we give ourselves over to another body of language opening onto another world of signifiers. I only know that we must speak (or just love) at least two languages to know that we are speaking one, that it is a language that we are speaking, and that an exile has both the chance and the nostalgia for understanding, in body and soul, that there is for him or her a tongue that is more maternal than the other. Hence Arendt's emotion when she hears German on the street upon her return to Germany for a few months between 1949 and 1950 as a representative for the Jewish Cultural Association.

Not only can one invent otherwise in another language, but one can invent in the place between-two-languages. That is called translating. Man is not an animal endowed with *logos*; he is a polyglot animal. Arendt makes philosophy out of the plurality of languages not by means of their so-called ontological hierarchy and not by respecting their so-called native and national integrity, as in Heidegger, but through the fact (I underscore *fact*) of their plurality: after Babel and with joy.[41] In November 1950, she gives a title to a page of the *Denketagebuch* she had begun in June: "*Pluralität der Sprachen*," "Plurality of languages." This passage is written in German, though I give it here in translation.

> Plurality of languages: *if there were only one language, we would perhaps be more assured about the essence of things.*
>
> What is determining is that (1) there are many languages and they are distinguished not only by their vocabulary but equally by their grammar, that is to say, essentially by their manner of thinking, and that (2) all languages can be learned.
>
> Given that the object, which is there to support the presentation of things, can be called "Tisch" as well as "table" *indicates that something of the genuine essence of things that we make and name escapes us.* It is not the senses and the possibilities for illusion that they contain that render the world uncertain, any more than it is the imaginable possibility or lived fear that everything is a dream. *It is rather the equivocity of meaning given within language and, above all, with languages.* At the heart of a homogenous human community, the essence of the table is unequivocally indicated by the word "table," and yet from the moment that it arrives at the frontier of the community, it falters.
>
> *This faltering equivocity of the world and the insecurity of the human that inhabits it would naturally not exist if it wasn't possible to learn foreign languages*, a possibility that demonstrates that there exist still other "correspondences" than ours in view of a common and identical world or even if only one language were to exist. Hence the absurdity of a uni-

versal language—it is against the "human condition," the artificial and all-powerful uniformization of equivocity.[42]

Arendt is polyglot as both a refugee and a theoretician of the political. The plurality of languages is a determining factor in the constitution of the world because, far from expressing in a different manner the same thing, as is commonly thought, the plurality of languages places difference at the heart of the essence of things. The reason for this is to be found, as Humboldt analyzes it for Greek and Basque, and as Benjamin repeatedly shows in "The Task of the Translator," as much in the modulations of semantics ("vocabulary," Arendt says) as in—and especially—the syntactical structure that informs the apperception of the world ("their grammar, that is to say, essentially their manner of thinking").[43] But there is a change in affect from Humboldt to Arendt. For him, it is a matter of "a growth in the richness of the world and the diversity of what we know about it," an expansion of "the region of human existence" so that "new ways of thinking and feeling are offered to us with determinate and real characteristics."[44] For her, it is a matter of "the faltering equivocity of the world and the insecurity of the human that inhabits it." "To learn foreign languages" is the condition of this philosophical, political, and existential trembling. It is "the equivocity of meaning" that produces "the faltering equivocity of the world": as if different languages, not unlike homonyms, were so many ways of producing things that are always different from themselves, the feeling of danger then coming from a homonymy that makes meaning tremble.[45] I would readily attribute the difference in affect, which is positive right from the start for Humboldt and more ambiguous for Arendt, to the difference between cosmopolitanism and exile. This is reflected in the way they go about classifying things: he thinks the difference between languages as a fact of synonymy, and she, as a fact of homonymy.[46]

What is most remarkable is that the equivocity is not simply located between languages, from one language to the other, but within a single language—"even if only one language were to exist," she says. The *Dictionary of Untranslatables* has taught me to see the pertinence of the remark invented by Jacques Lacan in "*L'Étourdit*" with regard to the languages of the unconscious, though it is also valid, it seems to me, for every language: "One language, among others, is nothing more than the totality of the equivocations that its history has allowed to persist in it."[17] Languages do not correspond to each other, for each language mobilizes other echoes, other "*correspondances*," as Arendt says in French, thinking of Baudelaire, so that a single language does not exactly say what it says: *trapeza* is also a bank in modern Greek, *mesa* is also a plateau in Castile or in the Andes. And always the signifier, sound and rhythm, returns in the semantic halo and the way of presenting things—*Tisch*, "*der Gegenstand, der für das tragende Präsentieren von Dingen da ist*," the "table," defined as the object that is used to "support the presentation of things,"[48] in Hannah's German, where the lexicon of phenomenology competes in the background with that of scholasticism.

Exiles, the Vanguard of the Human Condition

What, then, is the link between identity—Jewish, woman—and language, the languages of exile? The articulation between them now seems readily discernible: "The faltering equivocity" has become a model; for once, the exiles, the refugees, the Jews, are the vanguard of the "human condition." In the end, they embody the least absurd norm.

"At the frontier of the community," the word "falters": all the better! There is an optimism in Arendt that is consonant, in the end, with that of Humboldt: it consists in articulating the correspondences "in view," as she says, "of a common and identical world."[49] We must understand that the world in which we can "live together" is not a point of departure but a point of arrival, even a regulative principle. This world is politically constructed in particular via—or, perhaps we should say, in the full sense of the term *via*, "for example"—the possibility of learning a foreign language, in spite of/because of the faltering equivocity of the world and the insecurity of the person who inhabits it. This would be good politics: against a "uniformization" that runs the risk of totalitarianism, let us choose to complicate radically philosophical universality and truth. From nostalgia

to faltering equivocity: let the essence vacillate! Not to be assured of the
essence of things is the best thing that can happen to the world and to us.

One might find it strange that this condition, this "human condition,"
which Arendt puts in quotation marks, is revealed to us through a reflec-
tion on the languages of exile, on refugees and Jewish history. "We don't
like to be called 'refugees,'" she writes in 1943: "we ourselves call each
other 'newcomers' or 'immigrants'" ("WR" 264). Our newspapers—Arendt
wrote, recall, a column for the newspaper *Aufbau*,[50] though "We Refugees," the text from which I am drawing these lines, was published in Janu-
ary 1943 in the *Menorah Journal*—are destined for "Americans of German
language." Dark times: "Apparently nobody wants to know that contemporary history has created a new kind of human beings—the kind that are put
in concentration camps by their foes and in internment camps by their
friends" ("WR" 265).

Today, then, exiles, refugees, Jews, are no longer the excluded but models: "Refugees driven from country to country represent the vanguard of
their peoples—if they keep their identity. For the first time Jewish history
is not separate but tied up with that of all other nations" ("WR" 274).
There is nothing strange about this, in fact, "since society has discovered
discrimination as the great social weapon by which one may kill men without any bloodshed; since passports or birth certificates, and sometimes
even income tax receipts, are no longer official papers but matters of social
distinction" ("WR" 273). We shouldn't be surprised, then, that "young
African-Americans leaving the museum in Washington often say, 'We
didn't know the Jews were Black.'"[51] This is echoed by Arendt's curt words
in "Reflections on Little Rock": "as a Jew I take my sympathy for the cause
of the Negroes as for all oppressed and underprivileged people for granted
and should appreciate it if the reader did likewise."[52]

Will the "as" of assignation and reaction have contributed to a common
world? That remains to be shown. But we can affirm with some force that
there is, at present, nostalgia for this common world. Perhaps there can
only be nostalgia for this world. It is in this way that Europe might serve as
a model or paradigm. To cite Günther Anders again, writing from South-
ampton, in 1950:

That's what going home means: to leave behind our parents' remains; to stumble in the ruins of a city we have never seen; to arrive in a city and a country we have never known; to pay our respect to the vestiges of a past that is not our own. And yet we are at home. Not only because, for someone who comes from the US, England is already Europe, but because one is everywhere at home there where innocent victims have succumbed. (*JE* 112)

What is a European? Someone who is nostalgic for Europe.

Airborne Roots

Nostalgia. The right of return. To return home is a right. Everyone has the right to return. Resolution 194 of the United Nations, adopted on December 11, 1948, resolves that "refugees wishing to return to their homes and live at peace with their neighbors should be permitted to do so at the earliest practicable date." The "Law of Return" was voted on July 5, 1950, by the Knesset in order to guarantee immigration to Israel to any Jew and his or her family, even if non-Jewish. On November 22, 1974, the General Assembly of the United Nations adopted Resolution 3236, which reaffirms "the inalienable right of the Palestinians to return to their homes and property from which they have been displaced and uprooted, and calls for their return."

Günther Anders tells us that he "discovered one day in the New York Public Library an old treaty on *Morbus Helveticus* (homesickness)" and that he felt all the symptoms: "during the fourteen years I spent in America, not a day went by without my feeling nostalgic for my last European homeland: Paris."[53] He experiences every aspect of this feeling. The relationship between space and time: "the logic of the heart: the identification of the past with the house of the time before and with the world from before; or, rather, the idea of their original unity, not yet divided into two branches, 'time' and 'space.'" He knows that "it is a deadly disease" but "one that can be quickly cured by leading the patient to the 'fulfillment of his desires,' if only for a short while," probably because perception does not have the power to compete with nostalgia and the image it projects: "nostalgia, especially the type that has worsened over the years to the point that it has become a disease, had sketched out the 'essence.' What perception offers is too contingent, all too contingent. In truth, a single glance, the first one, is enough." Nostalgia is doubly unsettling: "the real, the shadow of the image," "What makes us indignant is not what has changed, but what has remained the same." We do not know if the worst is that everything has changed or that everything is still there. At home? "I would thus be 'back'? But the country to which I have 'returned' is not a country where I have ever lived," he writes in Vienna in May 1950. Flying over Berlin at last, on June 18, 1953, like Odysseus on the shores of Ithaca: "We'd dreamt about this return a thousand times. So hard to conceive: this extremely strange something—by comparison, the least known city seems familiar—that must be it over there, our home, with a gaze that takes it all in, a reunion." And on the 19th, at home not at home, this double nostalgia: "'What's up there?' someone asks passing behind the stranger. . . . He continues on his way, stranger than he had ever been in the most foreign of lands. He is punished for having refused these foreign countries: his at-home, here, has been denied to him."

But the lines that sum it all up for me are the ones he wrote in Vienna in December 1950: "We all know that our mother is mortal. But none of us knows that our home is mortal." Having been instructed by this syllogism of a new sort, we set out again with an oar on our shoulder.

To say that exile is the model for our contemporary human condition, to say that we are all exiles, is obviously a lot easier when you are not one yourself, or not really. Nostalgia, says Bolzinger, is "a cultural disease affecting the patrimony."[54] When the only patrimony is language, and when we make a profession of it, we can raise it up into the air and praise not uprootedness (for someone would then praise rootedness, in the worst way with Heidegger, in the best with Simone Weil) but airborne roots. "We change villages every day, and we continue working on the same text, whatever it is; at least, we try to. As to knowing whether what we write can take root, roots deeper than the filaments suspended in the air, that is another question" (*JE* 213). Culture removed from the land [*hors-sol*] is the right expression. In Brecht's *Conversations in Exile,* Ziffel (the tall burly physician with white hands) has just made the following remark to Kalle (the stocky one with the hands of a metal worker) regarding "patriotism": "One thing has always seemed strange to me: that one should have to love the country where one pays taxes. The foundation for patriotism is thus knowing how to be content with little: an excellent quality when one has nothing." And Kalle responds, "They always say that you have to have roots somewhere. I am convinced that the only beings to have roots, that is, trees, would rather not have any. They too would then be able to take a plane."[55] Indeed, man's character is not to be "rooted in the ground" (Epictetus, *Discourses*, III, 24, 12).[56] And since this is the case, I choose to understand that it is the tree of the bed that is rooted, not Odysseus himself. Odysseus is truly *polutropos,* with more than one ruse and more than one side. Yes, he longs for return, *oikade,* "home," but in the present moment he does not recognize his island; it is frightening, disturbingly uncanny in its very familiarity. And he leaves again right away, headed for the extreme elsewhere, at the end of the world.

I thus choose to understand, as the lesson of an odyssey, that we cannot stay "there," that is to say, that we "are" never "there," never at home. Rather than cultivating roots, I would cultivate the elsewhere, a world that does not close itself off, full of the "likes" of us, all different—like us, not like us.

When are we ever at home? When we are welcomed, we ourselves along with those who are close to us, together with our language, our languages.

Notes

OF CORSICAN HOSPITALITY

1. Arthur Rimbaud, "Eternity," in *Rimbaud: Complete Works, Selected Letters: A Bilingual Edition*, trans. Wallace Fowlie (Chicago: University of Chicago Press, 2005), 187.

2. René Goscinny and Albert Uderzo, *Asterix in Corsica*, trans. Anthea Bell and Derek Hockridge (London: Orion, 2004), 20.

3. A Corsican word meaning pointed or high-pitched, *pinzutu* is used to characterize the accent of the French from the mainland and especially from Paris. —Trans.

4. At the beginning of the twentieth century, Trieste, which had been part of Austria since 1382, became one of the main seats of the "irredentist" movement that sought the annexation to Italy of all lands that had historically been inhabited by Italians. —Trans.

5. See, for example, after Milman Parry, Moses Finley's *The World of Odysseus* (New York: NYRB, 2002).

6. *La patrie* can be translated into English both by *homeland* or *fatherland*. Depending on the context, I opt for one or the other. For example, when Aeneas is said to be leaving Troy with his father, Anchises, on his shoulders, *la patrie* lends itself more readily to *fatherland*. I also opt for *fatherland* when *langue maternelle* (mother tongue) and *patrie* are being discussed together. —Trans.

7. Jacques Derrida, *Learning to Live Finally*, trans. Pascale-Anne Brault and Michael Naas (Hoboken, N.J.: Melville House, 2007), 38.

8. The line is from Charles Baudelaire, "The Voyage," in *The Poems and Prose Poems of Charles Baudelaire*, trans. Francis Scarfe (New York: Brentano's, 1919), 88. —Trans.

9. See André Bolzinger, *Histoire de la nostalgie* (Paris: Éditions Campagne Première, 2007), which shows how Hofer's thesis (sixteen pages in 1688) was edited and "completed" by Zwinger (1710) and then reedited by Haller (1745), who returns to the original text but with an error in the date (1678 instead of 1688)—whence the hypothesis of a precursor by the name of Harder. See, also, on the relationship to medicine, Jean Starobinski's article "The Idea of Nostalgia," trans. William S. Kemp, *Diogenes* 14 (June 1966): 81–103, which is developed in his chapter "La leçon de la nostalgie" in *L'encre et la mélancolie* (Paris: Éditions du Seuil, 2012), 257–280.

10. Jean-Jacques Rousseau, *A Complete Dictionary of Music*, trans. William Warning (New York: AMS, 1975), 266–267.

11. The complete line reads: "Heureux qui comme Ulysse, a fait un beau voyage," "Happy, the man who finds sweet journey's end, Like Odysseus." Joachim du Bellay, *The Regrets: A Bilingual Edition*, trans. David R. Slavitt (Evanston, Ill.: Northwestern University Press, 2004), *Regret* 31, 77.

12. Cf. *The Dictionary of Untranslatables: A Philosophical Lexicon*, ed. Barbara Cassin, trans. Steven Rendall, Christian Hubert, Jeffrey Mehlman, Nathanael Stein, and Michael Syrotinski (Princeton, N.J.: Princeton University Press, 2014), in which all of these words have an entry.

13. Milan Kundera, *The Art of the Novel*, trans. Linda Asher (New York: Harper & Row, 1988), 128.

ODYSSEUS AND THE DAY OF RETURN

1. Homer, *The Odyssey*, trans. Richard Lattimore (Chicago: University of Chicago Press, 1951), XIX, 85. It is Odysseus as a foreign beggar who talks about Odysseus to Penelope. The same adjective is used for Telemachus, who has gone in search of his father: he is *nostimos* (IV, 806). *Nostos* is the key to the poem: "Glorious Odysseus, what you are after is sweet homecoming," Tiresias tells him in Hades (XI, 100); Athena says this about Ithaca to Odysseus: "your godlike wife . . . grieves over your homecoming" (XIII, 378–379); the diviner who wanted to marry Penelope sought to keep at bay "the end that sweet homecoming is" (Odysseus kills him with the rest) (XXII, 310). "Have they stopped believing in my return?" is the anguished question Odysseus keeps asking himself.

2. I use, though sometimes with modifications for a more literal rendering, Victor Bérard's beautiful translation (Paris: Éditions Armand Colin,

1931; Paris: Éditions Les Belles Lettres, 1972), from which Paul Demont and Marie-Pierre Noël have erased the interventionist flights of fancy (Paris: Éditions Livre de Poche, 1996), as well as Philippe Jacottet's (Paris: Éditions Maspero, 1982). In short, I retranslate.

3. René Char, "Pause at Cloaca Castle," in *The Brittle Age: and, Returning Upland*, trans. Gustaf Sobin (Denver, Colo.: Counterpath, 2009), 111. This phrase was written under a small Braque painting that Char described in this way: "Sisyphus as a bird, pushing his cloud of a rock" (*Sisyphe oiseau poussant son rocher nuage*).

4. Friedrich Nietzsche, *Human, All Too Human, I*, trans. Gary Handwerk (Stanford, Calif.: Stanford University Press, 1995), 180.

5. Friedrich Nietzsche, *The Birth of Tragedy*, trans. Douglas Smith (New York: Oxford University Press, 2000), 24–29.

6. To understand the meaning of *aiōn*, which designates all the vital liquids, tears, blood, sperm, and sweat, and thus also life, time allotted, duration, eternity, see Richard Broxton Onians, "The Stuff of Life," in *Philosophy of Plato and Aristotle* (New York: Arno, 1973), 200.

7. Immanuel Kant, *Anthropology from a Pragmatic Point of View*, ed. Hans H. Rudnick, trans. Victor Lyle Dowdell (Carbondale: Southern Illinois University Press), 69. "Later, when they visit these places, they find their anticipation dampened and even their homesickness cured. They think that everything has drastically changed, but it is that they cannot bring back their youth."

8. Joachim du Bellay, *The Regrets: A Bilingual Edition*, trans. David R. Slavitt (Evanston, Ill.: Northwestern University Press, 2004), *Regret* 31, 77; translation modified. —Trans.

9. I use this scene as my point of departure in *Comment faire vraiment des choses avec les mots*, forthcoming with Fayard. [See Barbara Cassin, "Sophistics, Rhetorics, and Performance; or, How to Really Do Things with Words," trans. Andrew Goffey, *Philosophy and Rhetoric* 42, no. 4 (2009): 349–372. —Trans.]

10. Sigmund Freud, "The Uncanny," in *The Standard Edition of the Complete Psychological Works of Sigmund Freud*, vol. 17, *1917–1919: An Infantile Neurosis and Other Works*, trans. James Strachey (London: Hogarth, 1958), 219.

11. The Greek terms are quite emphatic: *ithakēs hedos*, the site of Ithaca (XIII, 344); *khthōn*, the land (XIII, 352); *gaiēi*, the earth (XIII, 354); *zeidōron arouran*, the grain-giving ground (XIII, 354).

12. Cf. the article *"Mêtis"* in *The Dictionary of Untranslatables: A Philosophical Lexicon*, ed. Barbara Cassin, trans. Steven Rendall, Christian Hubert, Jeffrey Mehlman, Nathanael Stein, and Michael Syrotinski (Princeton, N.J.: Princeton University Press, 2014), esp. the boxed text "Ulysses: 'My name is no-body,' the first dramatization of *mêtis*," 658.

13. Parmenides, cited in *The Presocratic Philosophers*, ed. G. S. Kirk and J. E. Raven (Cambridge: Cambridge University Press, 1957), 276; these lines from Parmenides' poem (VIII, 26–34) echo the *Odyssey*, XII, 158–164. I develop this comparison in *Parménide, sur la nature ou sur l'étant. Le grec, langue de l'être?* (Paris: Éditions du Seuil, 1998), 53–60.

14. Or, rather, one more moment of recognition before the very last one, which is that of Laertes, Odysseus's father, whom Odysseus will see last in his garden, as flea-ridden as his dog: the sure signs are the thirteen pear trees, the ten apple trees, the forty fig trees, and the vine stocks that the father had given to him as a child.

15. One can hear the echo between the stupor evoked by the tomb, *taphos* (XXIII, 93), and the blow that strikes Penelope, *tethepen* (XXIII, 105).

16. The phrase *aspasios gē nēkhomenoisi* (XIII, 233) was deleted by the French translator Bérard. It is usually the woman who represents the homeland, like Elfriede Heidegger, who laments: "You are looking for your 'homeland' [*patrie*] in other women—alas, Martin—what has become of me?" Cited in *Ma chère petite âme: Lettres de Martin Heidegger à sa femme Elfriede: 1915–1970* (Paris: Éditions du Seuil, 2007), 406.

17. André Bolzinger, *Histoire de la nostalgie* (Paris: Éditions Campagne Première, 2007), 16–17.

18. *Odyssey*, XI, 121–137, where Odysseus makes Tiresias speak directly; and here, XXIII, 267–284, where Odysseus speaks of this to Penelope.

19. Lattimore too chooses to translate *ex halos* by "from the sea." —Trans.

20. *Odyssey*, III, 266, quoted by Bolzinger (*Histoire de la nostalgie*, 59), who later warns us that "equating the obsession of the return home when you are elsewhere with the desire to go elsewhere when you are at home is the abstract fruit of a logic born of a library" (213).

21. Parmenides: "[the way] on which mortals wander knowing nothing, two-headed; for helplessness guides the wandering thought in their breasts." VI, lines 5–6; cited in Kirk and Raven, *The Presocratics*, 271.

22. Emmanuel Levinas, "The Trace of the Other," trans. Alphonso Lingis, in *Deconstruction in Context*, ed. Mark Taylor (Chicago: University of Chi-

cago Press, 1986), 348. Cited by Ruedi Imbach in *Dante, la philosophie et les laïcs. Initiation à la philosophie médiévale* (Paris: Éditions du Cerf), 216.

23. Imbach, *Dante, la philosophie et les laïcs*, 244.

24. I am combining in my own way something from Vladimir Jankélévitch (*L'irréversible et la nostalgie* [Paris: Flammarion, 1974]) with Bolzinger and Imbach.

25. "'Let us flee, then, to the beloved Fatherland'—this would be the truer counsel. [To flee] as Odysseus ordered flight . . . Our Fatherland is There whence we have come, and There is the Father. What then is our course, what the manner of our flight?" Plotinus, *Ennead*, I, 6, 8; cited by Pietro Pucci in *Odysseus Polutropos: Intertextual Readings in the* Odyssey *and the* Iliad (Ithaca, N.Y.: Cornell University Press, 1987), 127. St. Maximus of Turin: "If, then, the story says of Odysseus that having been bound to the mast saved him from danger, how much more ought there to be preached what really happened—namely, that today the tree of the cross has snatched the whole human race from the danger of death." Sermon 37 in *The Sermons of St. Maximus of Turin*, trans. Boniface Ramsey (New York: Newman, 1989), 90; cited by Imbach in *Dante, la philosophie et les laïcs*, 227. For various Neoplatonic representations of this, Imbach refers to W. Beierwaltes, *Denken des Einen. Studien zur neoplatonischen Philosophie und ihrer Wirkungsgeschichte* (Frankfurt: Klostermann, 1985).

26. Levinas, "The Trace of the Other," 346.

27. *Sehnen, Trieb, Bedürfnis, Unbehagen*, and *Leere* are the terms used in Fichte's *Science of Knowledge* (1794–1797), *Gesamtausgabe der Bayerischen Akademie der Wissenschafte*, ed. Reinhard, Stuttgart-Bad Cannstadt, Frommann-Holzboog (1962), vol. I/2, 430ff. Cited in C. Helmreich's entry "Sehnsucht, Sehen" in the *Dictionary of Untranslatables*, 938–940.

28. Max Horkheimer and Theodor W. Adorno, *Dialectic of Enlightenment: Philosophical Fragments*, ed. Gunzelin Schmid Noerr, trans. Edmund Jephcott (Stanford, Calif.: Stanford University Press, 2002), 35. See Barbara Cassin, *Sophistical Practice: Toward a Consistent Relativism* (New York: Fordham University Press, 2014), 62–64.

29. Günther Anders, *Die Schrift an der Wand: Tagebücher 1941 bis 1966* (Munich: C. H. Beck, 1967), and *Tagebücher und Gedichte* (Munich: C. H. Beck, 1985). Published in French as *Journaux de l'exil et du retour*, "Revoir et oublier," trans. I. Kalinowski (Paris: Fage Éditions, 2012), 129. [Since there exists no published English translation of this text, and since the French edition is much

more comprehensive than the German edition, I have translated directly from
the French edition that Cassin cites throughout. —Trans.]

AENEAS: FROM NOSTALGIA TO EXILE

1. Virgil, *The Aeneid*, trans. James H. Matinband (New York: Frederick
Ungar, 1964).

2. André Bolzinger, *Histoire de la nostalgie* (Paris: Éditions Campagne
Première, 2007), 261.

3. Cicero, *De Inventione*, trans. H. M. Hubbell (Cambridge, Mass.:
Harvard University Press, 1949), II, 66; Cicero, *De Natura Deorum*, trans.
H. Rackham (Cambridge, Mass.: Harvard University Press, 1933) I, 41.
See also B. Collot's entry on "*Pietas*" and C. Auvray-Assayas's entry on
"*Religio*" in the *Dictionary of Untranslatables: A Philosophical Lexicon*, ed.
Barbara Cassin, trans. Steven Rendall, Christian Hubert, Jeffrey Mehlman,
Nathanael Stein, and Michael Syrotinski (Princeton, N.J.: Princeton
University Press, 2014).

4. "Those on the other hand who carefully reviewed and so to speak
retraced (*tamquam relegerent*) all the lore of ritual were called 'religious' (*reli-
giosi*) from *relegere*" (Cicero, *De Natura Deorum*, II, 28, 72); "We are fastened
and bound to God by this bond of piety" (Lactantius, *The Divine Institutes*,
trans. Sister Mary Francis McDonald, O.P. [Washington, D.C.: Catholic
University of America Press, 1964], 318). Cf. Émile Benveniste, *Indo-
European Language and Society*, trans. Elizabeth Palmer (London: Faber and
Faber, 1973), 518–523.

5. *Aeneadasque meo nomen de nomine fingo* (III, 18).

6. *Pergamaque Iliacamque iugis hanc addidit arcem* (III, 336).

7. The Latin is so beautiful: *dum per mare magnum Italiam sequimur fugi-
entem et uoluimur undis* (V, 628–629).

8. *Hoc Ilium et hoec loca Troiam esse jubet* (V, 756–757).

9. I will refer often in what follows to Florence Dupont's remarkable
book *Rome, la ville sans origine* (Paris: Éditions Gallimard, 2011).

10. *Pictura inani* (I, 464).

11. I use, while modifying here, the translation of André Bellesort (Paris:
Éditions Les Belles Lettres, 1961).

12. VII, 68: the seer exclaims: "I see a stranger (*externus*) coming." And
then he says, "Seek not, my son, to marry your daughter to a man of the Latin

race. . . . From abroad shall sons-in-law come, to wed our women and make our name illustrious (*externi venient generi qui sanguine nostrum*)" (95–99).

13. VII, 568–572, what is nicely called the "Amata sophism."

14. Herodotus, I, 57–58; Dionysius of Halicarnassus, *The Roman Antiquities*, 90.

15. Dupont, *Rome, la ville sans origine*, 98.

16. Jacques Derrida, *Memoires for Paul de Man*, trans. Cecile Lindsay, Jonathan Culler, Eduardo Cadava, and Peggy Kamuf (New York: Columbia University Press, 1989), 15. This is taken up by Derrida in the "Prière d'insérer" inserted in *Le monolinguisme de l'autre* (Paris: Éditions Galilée, 1996). [The "Prière d'insérer" is not included in the English translation, *Monolingualism of the Other*, trans. Patrick Mensah (Stanford, Calif.: Stanford University Press, 1998) —Trans.]

17. Derrida, *Monolingualism of the Other*, 8.

18. Arnaldo Momigliano, *Alien Wisdom: The Limits of Hellenization* (Cambridge: Cambridge University Press, 1975), 12.

19. *Le Front National*, the National Front, is a right-wing political party in France. —Trans.

20. Plato, *Menexenus*, trans. Rev. R. G. Bury, (Cambridge, Mass.: Harvard University Press, 1929), 245c-d. See also, for additional nuances, my article "Barbariser / barbare," in *Aglaïa. Autour de Platon. Mélanges offerts à Monique Dixsaut*, ed. A. Brancacci, D. El Murr, and D. Taormina (Paris: Éditions Vrin, 2010), 201–209.

21. Dupont, *Rome, la ville sans origine*, 166.

22. The Ausonians, and particularly the Rutulians, make up the coalition fighting with Turnus. It is the equivalent of the Acheans fighting under the walls of Troy.

23. XII, 818–841 (my emphasis).

24. *Graeci capta ferum victorem cepit et artis intulit agresti Latio.* Horace, *Epistles*, trans. H. R. Fairclough (Cambridge, Mass.: Harvard University Press, 1926), II, 1, 156–157. On the relationship between the Greek and Latin languages, see *Façons de parler grec à Rome*, ed. F. Dupont and E. Valette-Cagnac (Paris: Éditions Belin, 2005). See also Hannah Arendt, who, in her entire work, values political Latin over Heidegger's philosophizing Greek. Cf. Barbara Cassin, *Sophistical Practice: Toward a Consistent Relativism* (New York: Fordham University Press, 2014), 164–188.

25. Dupont, *Rome, la ville sans origine*, 75, 79. I am referring to and paraphrasing here the entirety of Chapter 3.

26. Cicero, *Laws*, trans. C. W. Keyes (Cambridge, Mass.: Harvard University Press, 1928), II, ii, 5.

27. Seneca, *Ad Helviam matrem de consolatione*, in *Dialogues and Essays*, trans. John Davie (Oxford: Oxford University Press, 2007), vol. III, VI, 5. Seneca was exiled to Corsica at the beginning of Claudius's reign in 41 BCE, and he spent seven years on the island.

28. Seneca, XI, 5.

29. Seneca, VII, 7. The key phrase: *romanum imperium nempe auctorem exsulem respicit.*

30. Seneca, VII, 5. *Quid aliud quam publica exsilia sunt?*

31. Ovid, *Tristia*, trans. L. R. Lind (Athens: University of Georgia Press, 1975), V, 12, 54–58. Ovid was *relegatus in perpetuum*, that is, placed under house arrest for life in Tomes (in what is today Romania) by Augustus, in 8 CE. He was, however, allowed to keep his fortune and rights.

32. Here is how Ovid's *Tristia* begins: "Little book, I don't begrudge it; you'll go to the City without me, Ay, to the place where your master isn't permitted to go! Off with you, but in disheveled dress as is proper for exiles; unhappy one, wear the clothes that befit my miserable state" (I, 1, 1–4).

ARENDT: TO HAVE ONE'S LANGUAGE FOR A HOMELAND

1. Hannah Arendt, "'What Remains? The Language Remains': A Conversation with Günter Gaus," in *Essays in Understanding, 1930–1954* (New York: Harcourt Brace & Company, 1994), 1–23; hereafter abbreviated as "LR."

2. This is her constant conviction: "A human being can defend himself only as the person he is attacked as. A Jew can preserve his human dignity only if he can be human as a Jew." Hannah Arendt, "A Way Toward the Reconciliation of Peoples," in *The Jewish Writings*, ed. Jerome Kohn and Ron H. Feldman (New York: Schocken, 2007), 261; hereafter abbreviated as *JW*.

3. "Belonging to Judaism had become my own problem, and my own problem was political. Purely political!" ("LR" 12). On this link between "Jew" and "Jewish" I refer the reader to "We Refugees," in *The Jewish Writings*, 264–274; hereafter abbreviated as "WR." She writes, for example: "It is the history of a hundred and fifty years of assimilated Jewry who performed an unprecedented feat: though proving all the time their non-Jewishness,

they succeeded in remaining Jews all the same" ("WR" 273). For a similar thought along the lines of gender identity, see my article "La perméabilité des genres: femme/philosophe, une identité stratégique," *Revue des femmes-philosophes*, UNESCO, no. 1 (November 2011), http://unesdoc.unesco.org/images/0021/002131/213131f.pdf#213158.

4. "I neither feel like a philosopher, nor do I believe that I have been accepted in the circle of philosophers. . . . The expression 'political philosophy,' which I avoid, is extremely burdened by tradition. . . . [The philosopher] cannot be objective or neutral with regards to politics. Not since Plato!" ("LR" 1–2). See, also, my *Sophistical Practice: Toward a Consistent Relativism* (New York: Fordham University Press, 2014), 164–167.

5. "The Jew as Pariah: A Hidden Tradition," in *JW*, 275–302.

6. Unpublished and untitled talk given at the Rand School in 1948, cited by Elisabeth Young-Bruehl, *Hannah Arendt: For Love of the World* (New Haven, Conn.: Yale University Press, 1982), 210; hereafter abbreviated as *HA*.

7. I develop this topic in "*Les langues de l'exil ou 'la chancelante équivocité du monde,'*" in *Portraits de l'exil, Paris-New-York, Dans le sillage d'Hannah Arendt, Photographie de Fred Stein* (Paris: Musée du Monparnasse/Arcadia Éditions, 2011), 11–26.

8. The French translation of this title is "Seule demeure la langue maternelle," that is, "Only the mother tongue remains." —Trans.

9. See Derrida's long note in *The Monolingualism of the Other*, trans. Patrick Mensah (Stanford, Calif.: Stanford University Press, 1998), 78–93, in which he compares the German of Rosenzweig to that of Arendt and that of Levinas.

10. This is Mary McCarthy's description of Arendt in a public lecture from the mid-1940s, cited by Elisabeth Young-Bruehl in *Hannah Arendt*, 199. —Trans.

11. From a letter dated July 6, 1967, thanking Ernst Johann, general secretary of the *Deutsche Akademie für Sprache und Dichtung*, which awarded Arendt the Sigmund Freud Prize for her scientific writings. This letter is quoted by Sylvie Courtine-Denamy in *Journal de pensée*, trans. Sylvie Courtine-Denamy (Paris: Éditions du Seuil, 2005), 1063.

12. Günther Anders, *Die Schrift an der Wand: Tagebücher 1941 bis 1966* (Munich: C. H. Beck, 1967), and *Tagebücher und Gedichte* (Munich: C. H. Beck, 1985). Published in French as *Journaux de l'exil et du retour*, "Revoir et oublier,"

trans. I. Kalinowski (Paris: Fage Éditions, 2012), 105–107, hereafter abbreviated as *JE*.

13. Friedrich Schleiermacher, *Hermeneutics and Criticism, and Other Writings*, trans. Andrew Bowie (Cambridge: Cambridge University Press, 1998), 229.

14. [In English in the original. —Trans.] The words from the mother tongue that "we use in ordinary speech receive their specific weight, the one that guides our usage and saves it from mindless clichés, through the manifold associations which arise automatically and uniquely out of the treasure of great poetry in which that particular language and no other has been blessed." Hannah Arendt, *Responsibility and Judgment* (New York: Schocken, 2003), 5. This speech was delivered by Hannah Arendt upon receiving Denmark's Sonning Prize in 1975. Elisabeth Young-Bruehl quotes in its entirety this long, heavy sentence, which I have cut up, and characterizes it as "Germanic English" (*HA* xiv).

15. Hannah Arendt, *Eichmann in Jerusalem: A Report on the Banality of Evil* (New York: Penguin, 1963), 48; hereafter abbreviated as *EJ*.

16. Aristotle, *Politics*, trans. H. Rackham (Cambridge, Mass.: Harvard University Press, 1932), I, i, 10, 1253a.

17. Hannah Arendt, *Denktagebuch*, 2 vols. (Munich: Piper, 2003), vol. 2, November 1965 [58], 642–643; French translation, *Journal de pensée*, trans. Sylvie Courtine-Denamy, vol. 2, November 1965 [58], 837–838. Hence the rather strange result that one "instantaneously destroys the objects of thought" as soon as one tries to reduce language to a mathematical language, a result that then extends to the natural sciences: "Since the natural sciences *no longer express themselves in their native language*, their objects have stopped being objects of thought. They are constantly trying to 'think the unthinkable,' which is manifestly impossible. They have created some 'unthinkable' and are trying to apprehend it after the fact through thought." (My emphasis)

18. Plato, *Protagoras*, trans. W. R. M. Lamb (Cambridge, Mass.: Harvard University Press, 1924), 328a: "Why, you might as well ask who is a teacher of Greek [*hellēnizein*]; you would find none anywhere." See also 325cff.

19. Isocrates, *Panegyricus*, in *Isocrates*, trans. George Norlin (Cambridge, Mass.: Harvard University Press, 1928), 50: "And so far has our city distanced the rest of mankind in thought and in speech that her pupils have

become the teachers of the rest of the world; and she has brought it about that the name 'Hellenes' suggests no longer a race (*genous*) but an intelligence (*dianoias*), and that the title 'Hellenes' is applied rather to those who share our culture (*tēs paideuseōs*) than to those who share a common blood (*tēs koinēs phuseōs*)."

20. Martin Heidegger, *The Essence of Human Freedom: An Introduction to Philosophy*, trans. Ted Sadler (New York: Continuum, 2002), 35–36. A note at the end of the sentence indicates: "Cf. Master Eckhart and Hegel." It is I who have emphasized the line: "*Der Grad bemisst sich nach der Tiefe und Gewalt der Existenz des Volkes und Stammes, der die Sprache spricht und in ihr existiert.*"

21. I am borrowing the term "ontological nationalism" and its diagnosis from the Germanist and translator Jean-Pierre Lefebvre.

22. Martin Heidegger, "Letter on Humanism," in *Basic Writings*, trans. David Farrell Krell (New York: Harper & Row, 1976), 213. And the beautiful finale, all the more striking for its simplicity: "In this way language is the language of Being, as clouds are the clouds of the sky" (242).

23. Heidegger, "Letter on Humanism," 217. This passage is used as an exergue by Pietro Pucci in *Odysseus Polutropos*. I am grateful to Jean-François Courtine for an exchange in which he communicated to me some of the following points, which I sometimes take up literally, even if I am reluctant to use them with benevolence when speaking of Heidegger.

24. Martin Heidegger, *Gesamtausgabe 39: Hölderlins Hymnen "Germanien" und "Der Rhein*," ed. Susanne Ziegler (Frankfurt am Main: Vittorio Klostermann, 1980), 121; *Hölderlin's Hymns "Germania" and "The Rhine*," trans. William McNeill and Julia Ireland (Bloomington: Indiana University Press, 2014), 109. This line is cited by Emmanuel Faye in *Heidegger, l'introduction du nazisme dans la philosophie* (Paris: Éditions Albin Michel, 2005), 172.

25. Heidegger, *The Fundamental Concepts of Metaphysics: World, Finitude, Solitude* (Winter Semester Course, 1929–1930), trans. William McNeill and Nicholas Walker (Bloomington: Indiana University Press, 1995), 5–6. [The English translation of *Heimweh* is *homesickness* here, whereas Cassin uses *nostalgie*. —Trans.]

26. Martin Heidegger, *Introduction to Metaphysics*, trans. Ralph Manheim (New Haven, Conn.: Yale University Press, 1959), 151–152. And then, in *Parmenides*, Heidegger concludes: "Because the Greeks are utterly unpolitical

people . . . they could, and precisely had to, found the *polis*." Heidegger, *Parmenides*, trans. André Schuwer and Richard Rojcewicz (Bloomington: Indiana University Press, 1992), 96.

27. Heidegger, *Parmenides*, 89.

28. "I have always loved Greek poetry. And poetry has played a large role in my life" ("LR" 9).

29. Jacques Derrida, *Learning to Live Finally: The Last Interview*, trans. Pascale-Anne Brault and Michael Naas (Hoboken, N.J.: Melville House, 2007), 38. Derrida refers in this text to *The Monolingualism of the Other* for more details about his "singular history" as a "Jewish *pied-noir*" affected by the abolition of the Crémieux Decree.

30. *Denktagebuch*, vol. 1, August 1950 [21], 15–16; see *Journal de pensée*, vol. 1, August 1950 [21], 28–29.

31. *Denktagebuch*, vol. 1, November 1950 [16], 43. [This passage is written by Arendt in English in the *Denktagebuch*. —Trans.]

32. Günther Anders, "*Post festum*," in *Journaux de l'exil et du retour. Vienna, June 1951*, 236. I would like to invent here a term such as *deshommes* [somemen] to match Lacan's *lalangue*.

33. "Language manifests itself in reality exclusively as multiplicity." Wilhelm von Humboldt, *On Language. On the Diversity of Human Language Construction and Its Influence on the Mental Development of the Human Species*, ed. Michael Losonsky, trans. Peter Heath (Cambridge: Cambridge University Press, 1999). *Uber die Verschiedenheiten des menschlichen Sprachbaues*, in *Gesammelte Schriften*, ed. Albert Leitzmann et al. (Berlin: B. Behr, 1907), 6:240. Cited and translated in my *Sophistical Practice*, 310.

34. Hannah Arendt, *Within Four Walls: The Correspondence Between Hannah Arendt and Heinrich Blücher, 1936–1968*, ed. Lotte Kohler, trans. Peter Constantine (New York: Harcourt Inc., 2000), 6.

35. Victor Klemperer, *I Shall Bear Witness: The Diaries of Victor Klemperer, 1993–41*, trans. Martin Chalmers (London: Weidenfeld & Nicolson, 1998), 89.

36. Victor Klemperer, *The Language of the Third Reich*, trans. Martin Brady (London: Continuum, 2000), 14.

37. "Kant, *Self*—The 'I think' must accompany all my representations (. . .) This would be altogether incomprehensible if the self were a *One* and basta" (May 1970, XXVII, 52) [English in the original]; or "Machiavelli lehrt 'how not to be good,' weil goodness sich verbirgt" (March 1955, XXI, 9). Cited

by Sylvie Courtine-Denamy in "Dans l'atelier d'Hannah Arendt," *Journal de pensée*, vol. 2, 1065, 1064.

38. Elisabeth Young-Bruehl, *Hannah Arendt*, "Preface," l.

39. Allow me to refer to "Greeks and Romans: Paradigms of the Past in Arendt and Heidegger," in my *Sophistical Practice*, 164–188.

40. Elisabeth Young-Bruehl, *Hannah Arendt*, 199, 191.

41. This is how I sum up the problematic of the *Dictionary of Untranslatables: A Philosophical Lexicon*, ed. Barbara Cassin, trans. Steven Rendall, Christian Hubert, Jeffrey Mehlman, Nathanael Stein, and Michael Syrotinski (Princeton, N.J.: Princeton University Press, 2014).

42. Hannah Arendt, *Denktagebuch*, 2 vols. (Munich: Piper, 2003), [15], I, 42–43; *Journal de pensée*, II, November 1950, 56–57. Cited and translated in Barbara Cassin, "Sophistics, Rhetorics, and Performance; or, How to Really Do Things with Words," trans. Andrew Goffey, *Philosophy and Rhetoric* 42, no. 4 (2009): 368. My emphasis.

43. Cassin, "Sophistics, Rhetorics, and Performance," 368.

44. Wilhelm von Humboldt, "Fragment of a Monograph on the Basque," in *La langue source de la nation*, ed. Pierre Caussat, Dariusz Adamski, and Marc Crépon (Liege/Brussels: Mardaga, 1996), 433; see Barbara Cassin, "Sophistics, Rhetorics, and Performance; or, How to Really Do Things with Words," 366.

45. Cassin, "Sophistics, Rhetorics, and Performance," 368. Allow me to refer the reader to *La décision du sens*, authored with M. Narcy (Paris: Éditions Vrin, 1989), where I analyze the fundamental equivalency necessary to establishing the principle of noncontradiction: to speak is to signify something that has a meaning, indeed a single meaning, for oneself and for others. The prohibition of homonymy has been, since Aristotle, just as much a structuring element of language as the prohibition of incest has been for society.

46. Humboldt talks about a "synonymy of principal languages" in the introduction to his translation of Aeschylus's *Agamemnon* (cited in Cassin, "Sophistics, Rhetorics, and Performance," 366). I develop this theme in "Accident/accident de voiture," in *Compléments de substance. Études sur les propriétés accidentelles offertes à Alain de Libera*, ed. Ch. Erismann and A. Schniewind (Paris: Éditions Vrin, 2008), 19–32.

47. Jacques Lacan, "L'Etourdit," ed. Cormac Gallagher (2010), section 47, 20, http://www.lacaninireland.com/web/wp-content/uploads/2010/06/etourdit-Second-turn-Final-Version4.pdf.

48. Cassin, "Sophistics, Rhetorics, and Performance," 368.

49. Cassin, "Sophistics, Rhetorics, and Performance," 368.

50. *Aufbau* is a newspaper for German-speaking Jewish people throughout the world. It was created in 1934 by the German-Jewish Club. In 1939, its new director, Manfred George, turned it into one of the first anti-Nazi newspapers of the German press in exile. Published in New York until 2004, it now comes out in Zurich. The column written by Arendt for many years starting in 1941 bore the idiomatic English title: "This means you!"

51. Michael Berenbaum, project director of the Holocaust Museum in Washington, cited by Eva Ulrike Pirker in *Narrative Projections of a Black British History* (New York: Routledge, 2011), 45.

52. "Preliminary Remarks," *Dissent* (Winter 1959): 46; cited by Elisabeth Young-Bruehl in *Hannah Arendt*, 309.

53. Günther Anders, *Die Schrift an der Wand: Tagebücher 1941 bis 1966* (Munich: C. H. Beck, 1967). I am combining sentences from pages 196 (Vienna, November 1950), 115–116 (Paris, April 1950), 196 (Vienna, November 1950), 113 (Paris, April 1950), 138 (Wiener Wald, July 1950), 116 (Paris, April 1950), 125 (Vienna, May 1950), 262 (Berlin, June 18, 1953), 263 (Berlin, June 19, 1953), and 210 (Vienna, December 1950).

54. Bolzinger, *Histoire de la nostalgie*, 112.

55. Bertolt Brecht, *Dialogues d'exilés*, French trans. Gilbert Badia and Jean Baudrillard (Paris: Éditions de l'Arche, 1972), 78–79.

56. Epictetus, *The Discourses as Reported by Arrian*, trans. W. A. Oldfather (London: William Heinemann, 1928).

Library of Congress Cataloging-in-Publication Data

Cassin, Barbara.
[Nostalgie. English]
Nostalgia : when are we ever at home? / Barbara Cassin ;
translated by Pascale-Anne Brault ; foreword by Souleymane Bachir Diagne.
pages   cm
Includes bibliographical references.
ISBN 978-0-8232-6950-1 (hardback) — ISBN 978-0-8232-6951-8 (paper)
1. Homesickness in literature.   2. Nostalgia—Philosophy.   3. Homesickness.
4. Odysseus (Greek mythology)   5. Aeneas (Legendary character)
6. Arendt, Hannah, 1906–1975.   I. Brault, Pascale-Anne.   II. Title.
PN56.H563C3713   2016
809'.93353—dc23
2015028081